50 EASY

50 Easy Outreach Ideas

PAUL MOGFORD

EASTBOURNE

Published by
KINGSWAY PUBLICATIONS
Lottbridge Drove, Eastbourne, BN23 6NT, England.
E-mail: books@kingsway.co.uk

Designed and produced for the publishers by
Bookprint Creative Services, P.O. Box 827, BN21 3YJ, England.
Printed in Great Britain.

Contents

Acknowledgements

In writing such a book, there are many people that I need to thank for all sorts of reasons. First, I am particularly grateful to the leaders and members of Kings Church Eastbourne. The leaders have been significant in firing my desire to serve God both in the church and in reaching out to people in Eastbourne. This book is a result of their encouragement. Kings Church is an outward-looking and evangelistically minded church, and many of these ideas have been thought of and used by members of the church. I would like to thank all those who have directly contributed through ideas and those who have contributed indirectly through participation. Thanks also to my friends who have to put up with my quirks! Finally, thanks to my family who are God's visible blessing in my life.

Preface

Back to basics

This book is about reaching out to your friends, having fun with them and enjoying each other's company. I have attempted to bring together some of the ideas we have tried (and sometimes failed with!) at our church. Most of the ideas are pretty basic and for this I make no apology. A quick survey of local church groups showed that few people had any creative ideas on how to reach out to their community and friends, and yet all felt the need to reach beyond their own boundaries. For some churches outreach has become fixed on set-piece events or one-off special meetings. The thought of using a barbecue to invite non-Christian friends along as part of an evangelism programme has not yet crossed their minds, let alone taking people into the woods to shoot paint pellets at each other. Even now, many will ask what relevance such activities have to the gospel.

I hope that by suggesting the basics, and offering variations on them, many more churches will realize the resources they have, encourage their people to become more outward-looking and get on with the task of reaching out, while having fun on the way!

Bridging the gap

This book is not about evangelism – there are already many good resources on the subject and I am not best qualified to write about it. This book is primarily aimed at those Christians who feel that evangelism is too hard for them; that success only comes with hard effort and a three-point message; that only leaders can engage in evangelism.

In actual fact, most successful evangelism takes place in day-to-day routine and everyday friendship. So this book is for those who are looking for ideas to reach out to non-Christians in a non-threatening way with no strings attached. I hope it will offer the opportunity to try events and ideas that will not embarrass anyone and will be enjoyed by everyone.

These events are to be used as part of the journey in evangelism, not the end. What I mean is that most non-Christians are not queuing outside the church to become Christians – most are in fact at best ambivalent, though not hostile to the gospel. Using these events will help develop relationships and trust, leading to stronger opportunities for Christians to share their faith. Friendship evangelism was very much the buzzword some years ago, though in reality it has always been the best form of evangelism for the vast majority of Christians. We cannot all be Billy Graham or J. John, but we can all befriend other people.

In fact the most popular form of friendship evangelism already takes place week by week in the guise of Alpha courses. At the time of writing, Alpha has now drawn more than a million people, with startling results. In our own church, it has helped us reach out to more than 300 people, of which a good 100 have become Christians. Not all have stayed (that is the subject of another book), but many have. Church members have become excited that evangelism in this form does work. In addition, success breeds success.

However, Alpha is not the be all and end all of evangelism. It is only a tool in the armoury of the local church. This
book will help you plan events that, while fun in nature and
seemingly without a gospel presentation, will help you create
an environment in which strong relationships can be built
and trust can be established. Experience in our own church
has shown that the stronger the relationship, the more
effective the evangelism. The new Christian will become an
active local church participant more quickly and 'drop-out'
will be lower because strong ties are harder to break.

At the end of the day, though, while this book is about
outreach evangelism, it is foremost about friendship for
friendship's sake. People everywhere will run a mile if they
think that you are out to get them. If after all your attempts
your friend does not wish to become a Christian, does this
mean you must 'dump' them and move on to the next target?
God forbid! Friendship is about giving and trust, not about
results. It was said of Jesus that he was a friend of sinners,
and we should strive to be like him, befriending people and
reaching out in love.

How to Use This Book

The long term

It is important to have a long-term game plan. One meeting will simply not be enough. It has been estimated that most people need at least seven presentations of the gospel before they will respond. This holds true for relationships. Some years ago, my wife and I befriended a couple in similar circumstances to us. We met as couples, went to the theatre together, met as families, went for walks. We covered many other different social contexts. We became friends – we laughed together, cried together, ate together and had fun together. The subject of Christianity came up in casual conversation many times (often initiated by our friends), and it was clear that our friendship was not a hindrance to the gospel, nor was the gospel a hindrance to our friendship. Sadly, they never (to my knowledge) made the final steps to faith, but who knows what tomorrow will bring?

Different contexts allow other people to see what sort of person you really are. Many of us prefer our friends to see us at our best, our nicest and our kindest. After all, isn't this what Christians are supposed to be? I have often thought about the slogan 'Games that bring people together' on the

Monopoly box. Well, some of the gentlest caring people become monsters when they own Mayfair and Park Lane and you want to trade! Let people see the real you – that is what they are looking for. Paintballing can be a real eye-opening way to show the grace of God in your life!

So, think long term. Plan different settings and different events that will allow people to see different sides of you and your church. Be daring – try anything once. If it does not work, be honest and try something else. Most small groups can plan an event every six weeks. In between, invite the people who attend those events to your house for a meal or for drinks. If they have a family, perhaps you could invite them over for a video or go to the pictures together. Whatever you do, ensure that you continue to engage the people you contact. Do not summon up your courage to invite them to one event and then never speak to them again!

Some people are great at inviting non-Christians to an Alpha course or evangelistic events, but then do not engage them in a more relaxed atmosphere. Think about it. If the only context you have is work, you don't know their partners and you have not tried to get to know them socially, what chance have you got of getting them along to a full-blown gospel presentation? Ask yourself the question: 'How would I respond/feel given our current relationship?' Long-term planning will alleviate the problem and allow your Christian friends the opportunity to deepen and further relationships.

Planning the event

Most people in our society now live lives at a fast pace and plan well ahead. So must you. The adage 'Book now to avoid disappointment' is very true in this situation. Give yourself several weeks to plan and book venues. You will need time to think about who to invite; then you will need time to issue invitations and keep talking to your friends about the event. A one-off invite is not going to be sufficient. Too many people say that they have invited a friend to something, but in reality that friend has not registered the invitation and disappointment beckons. In fact you need to be talking about the event every week in your group in the run up. In turn, group members need to continue talking to those they have invited to make sure that they understand the date, time and nature of the event. If you do not believe me, ask your group what the notices were in church this week!

First discussions

I have written this book with a home or cell group, or planning group, in mind, rather than one lonely individual who tries to organize everything. Do not be autocratic about the event, making all the decisions yourself. While someone needs to take responsibility and give the discussion shape, all members of your group need to feel part of the decision-making process. You can always weed out the weaker suggestions, but nonetheless your group needs to engage with the event. Too many good ideas fall apart because the leader thought everyone was with him, when in fact only his wife was, and then out of embarrassment!

I strongly recommend that your very first event is one that is simple and easy to plan and execute. Over-elaboration at this point will put people off and give them cause for second thought next time (remember, success breeds success). Therefore, barbecues, ten-pin bowling and other simple everyday events are best to start with. When you are confident, go for something more elaborate, such as a football evening or a Mexican night.

Ask yourselves what you are able to do. If you have an elderly group, running around playing paintball may not be the wisest group activity! Choose something in which the majority of your group can participate. Sometimes it is good to have a men only night, or a women only night, but do not always choose activities that are gender exclusive. The same goes for age-exclusive ideas.

Some ideas might need two or more groups to join together. Also, remember that not everyone has the same income as you do, so make sure that you have a mix of price-sensitive events (sometimes the free ones are the best!).

Finally, remember that your group has a mix of people with different needs and problems/opportunities. Make sure that over a period of time you address all those needs. Be sensitive to your group. If you have an ex-alcoholic in your group, going to the pub would be inadvisable. Similarly, if someone is on the dole or income supplement, they will always be excluded from costly events and their position will only be highlighted.

Commitment

Every member needs to be committed to what you are doing, even if they cannot come that night. Prayer is the obvious means of committing yourself to the event. Be careful that good intentions do not become the excuse for not coming ('I think that God is calling me to pray for you that night!'). It is easy to use prayer or other meetings as an excuse not to bother – there may be other reasons for not wanting to attend. Try to be honest with each other.

Be careful in your planning. The date is important. Our church once held a very good evangelistic outreach . . . on the same day as the FA Cup Final. As you can imagine, turnout was low! Unfortunately, the FA will not move their date to allow you to hold a well-attended event. Good planning will help you to avoid situations like this.

If money is involved, make sure that you get it before the event. This has two effects. First, only those who really intend to go will pay out before the event. Second, it means that you will not be out of pocket when some say, 'I've forgotten my money – again!' As a basic principle where money is involved, simply use the maxim 'No money – no go'.

Listen to your group. If there is too much hesitancy, attendance may not be great. On the other hand, you may need to push people to get their interest and attendance. This is a fine balance that only the group leader can assess.

Aims

What are your aims for the evening? Be very clear and write them down. In doing so, your aims will give a clear shape to your event. For example, if your aim is to have someone share his or her story, you need to allow time for this to happen. If it is to have a great time building relationships, planning some good icebreakers will be helpful. Do not assume anything – plan everything. Do not assume that simply putting non-Christians into the room with your house group will encourage your house group to talk to their guests. You must plan to help the conversation move ahead.

It is important to inform your house group of the level of spiritual input there will be at the event. It is highly embarrassing and unhelpful if the impression is given that the event is to be a fun night with no spiritual input only to find that you decided ('in the Spirit') to share a ten-minute gospel presentation. Guess how many people you will get along to the next event! You may wish to have a full-blown testimony and sharing night. But whatever you decide, do not tell your group one thing and do another, or they will quickly lose trust in you. Be true to your intentions and make it clear to your group what to expect (maybe by way of a simple leaflet). It will help them decide who to invite along.

Build a long-term aim into your thinking. The next event should really be in the pipeline before the first one has taken place. It gives your group an immediate follow-up with their guests. Striking while the iron is hot is a truism that you need to follow. One of our house groups recently had a successful cheese and wine evening with three guests, but their next event is not for another ten weeks, so any impetus has now been lost and will need work to recover. Do not keep trying to begin over and over again. Once impetus has been gained, keep it rolling. It is easier pushing a bus down the hill than up it!

Finally, you may want to invite a church member from outside your group to help. There will be people in your church who are good fishers of men. They are like magnets. Put them into a room of non-Christians and they will immediately be at home, chatting away and making everyone feel comfortable. Inevitably, these people will befriend someone and within weeks will be inviting them to Alpha. Use the gifts God has placed at your disposal. That is exactly why God put them in your church.

The gospel

There is only one gospel, but the presentation can be multiple. Sometimes the presentation can be direct and challenging. Sometimes it is subtle and gentle. Sometimes it is in words, sometimes in deed. It is important to understand that one style and approach does not do for all situations. Nor is one style appropriate for everyone. Everyone learns in different ways, although there are broadly four categories: imaginative, analytical, dynamic (problem-solving/creative) and common sense. *Learning Styles* by Marlene LeFevre is a great book to help you understand these principles. In effect, using different approaches will speak to these learning needs and make your outreach more appropriate. A single-style approach will only ever reach one group of people.

Further, following this approach will ensure that you are not just doing the things you enjoy. (By the way, if others suggest doing something you would not enjoy, it is your responsibility to put yourself into it with a full heart. If you don't, how can you ever expect your group to participate in activities they do not enjoy?) A mix will ensure that there is something for everyone, and a mix of approaches to the gospel will ensure that you reach different sorts of people.

The cost

Be sensitive about money. Money makes the world go round, but it also divides the haves from the have-nots. There will always be a tension about money, particularly in Christian circles. This is because many of us believe that we can propagate the gospel on the cheap, without financial cost to ourselves. In fact most of the events in this book are relatively inexpensive, but there are those that cost more. Be sensitive to the group's needs. As already stated, booking an expensive event highlights the problems of those in your group who cannot afford to participate. Therefore, you might need to subsidise some events or adapt them to your circumstances.

However, always be aware that there will be another cost: time. It will take time to cultivate relationships. It might mean that some of your group, you included, might have to forego some other treat to participate. It will take time for your non-Christian friends to trust your invites, and it will take time to follow up the events on a one-to-one and group basis. You must be prepared to put time into the events.

Facilities

Be aware of the facilities you need. Some events can be hosted in houses; others in church; yet others in special premises (playing Laser Quest at home would be interesting!). You must take responsibility to ensure that (a) the facilities are suitable for your event and (b) you have booked the appropriate facility for the right night at the right time. This should always be double checked. The success of the event and the trust of your group depend upon it. Don't assume anything. If you ask a group member to book something, check that it has been done (although do it in a way that does not undermine the individual – they may feel that you do not trust them if you ask them every day for a week!).

Food and drink

Eating together is by far the best and easiest way of getting to know people. The Bible is full of such examples, and the Alpha course is the best example in our times of how food helps to build relationships. Be creative, however. Pizza is wonderful, but it is not the be all and end all of culinary delights. Use food as a building-block, and allow time for people to enjoy it. Similarly with drinks. Be sensitive to the feelings of people around you. Alcohol is still a touchy subject in many churches and one that needs to be handled carefully. There are many enjoyable substitutes to alcohol.

Follow-up

Be prepared to follow up the people who actually attend your event through as many different ways as possible. These will include:

- *Individual meetings*. The best people to follow up on their guests are those who brought them along. Get them to arrange coffee or walks or any other 'normal' everyday events. They could even invite them round for a meal!

- *More events*. Make sure that you have more events lined up for them to ensure another contact.

- *Alpha*. If you have not already started an Alpha course, start one now. Make sure that you have something into which you can feed your contacts. This could be a Just Looking course, Alpha or another low-profile outreach event.

The press

All towns now have their own local newspaper and most have local radio. Many of them are desperate for news items or photo opportunities. You should really foster good relationships with your local media. Get to know them and the sort of stories they are looking for. You will find that if you dress your events up in the right way, you will get loads of free publicity both before and after. Our church is in the local newspapers most weeks because of one event or another. Even events that may seem mundane to you, such as a visiting speaker, can help fill newspaper columns! If you are able to get a local councillor involved, even better. Because they need to be re-elected, they are more than willing to get their photo in the newspaper and will encourage the newspaper to get involved!

Charities

Throughout the book I often mention getting involved with local charities. This can give your event some credibility, but you should not use a charity simply to get publicity. I personally feel very uncomfortable with the idea of involving a charity just because it can boost your appeal. Only get involved with charities you believe in. It is important to become involved with all sorts of charitable causes, but there are many demands on our time and money. Adopting one or two special charities, be they local or national, will be a means of benefitting people who need help and will give a focus to your giving.

Cell church

There has recently been much discussion about cell church and its impact and usefulness in the UK church. For further reading, I would recommend *The Second Reformation* by Bill Beckham. Essentially, cells are about relationships and opening up house groups to non-Christian friends and neighbours.

I have written this book in the context of a church that is currently moving to a cell structure, and I have used many of the activities either in my own cell or with a group of other cells. Some we have organized as a church. Each of the activities is designed to grow relationships with each other and with non-group members. Hopefully, many are fun, and they often include laughter and food. To my mind food and laughter are two very important factors in relationship in the early stages. From this, commitment and trust can be built over time.

Most cell books advocate the use of a harvest or outreach week. This usually takes place two or three times a year, and is a church-driven evangelism week. You can use these weeks in two ways. First, by hosting many events before the week, you can then focus on several major evangelistic meetings. You could use music or a special guest as a centrepiece (you will find it easier if there is a natural reason for this, for example Christmas or a baptismal service). The activities leading up to the week will be with the intent of inviting people along.

Alternatively, if your church is not really ready for such a major outreach week, you could use the week to host a number of cell-group outreach ideas, culminating in one or two larger activities such as a barn dance or quiz night. This could point towards an Alpha course, which would be starting very shortly afterwards.

Relationships

Regrettably, all too many Christians bemoan the fact that they do not know any non-Christians – or at least not well enough to invite to church. The truth is really somewhat different. Many church members, if pressed, do have non-Christian friends, people they know in the workplace, or have chatted to at the school gate. Perhaps they are acquaintances at the health club, or live next door. We are surrounded by people we either have a passing chat with, or invite into our lives and homes.

It is true, however, that we have become engaged with the Christian subculture to the point where we do not spend the quality time with others that is necessary to provide the basis for relationships. Going to the prayer meeting, youth meeting, Alpha, PCC or other worthy but time consuming church meetings seems to have robbed us of the time we could spend with others. We have to be careful that we are not falling into a trap of our own making. The Christian subculture and our friendships within it are often very comfortable and undemanding. We tie ourselves down in ministry or leadership activities and leave no room for people. Too often we allow church to become the be all and end all of our lives. Alternatively, we reject the subculture, somehow preferring to be with 'real' people, and we opt out of the calling God has placed on our lives, namely to be active and fruitful members of a local expression of the body of Christ.

Neither will do. In pursuing the first line, we fail to reach out to the very lost world from which we were rescued. Paul's words, 'How can they believe if they have not been told?', ring in our ears. Pursuing line two leaves us open to the possibility of stunted Christian growth, or worse, and without the necessary resources to establish our newly evangelized friends.

This book is primarily about relationships. It is about creating a context in which both the Christian and the non-Christian can meet without feeling either embarrassed or pressured in any way. Relationships can only be formed through spending time together. They cannot magically appear or be spontaneously created. We must also side-step or deal with the image most non-churched people have of us (see *Weird Christians I Have Met* by Philip Baker for some great parodies that exist). Creating fun contexts can show people that we are not some strange, alien beings; nor are we so straight-laced that their great great aunt Maud would have approved of us!

Finally, treat other people in the way you would wish to be treated. Anything that hints of you being out to get them will send them running a mile! As I said earlier, the basis for reaching out to people is to reach out to them in friendship. We must seek to make new disciples, but we must show interest in people because they are people, not because they are part of our global evangelism plan!

1 Art Afternoon

In many ways this event is not dissimilar to the *Blue Peter* idea: 'All you need is a box and some sticky-backed plastic!' Most people (of all ages) like to play with paints and other art materials. You will find adults and children alike having a great time together!

PLANNING

You will need to plan a fair way in advance (four to five weeks) as you may need to get materials together. These materials will depend upon the kind of afternoon you intend to have. For example, you could simply work with different sorts of paints and crayons. In that case you would need enough paints, crayons and paper for the number of people you invite. Alternatively, you could design one huge mural (like the Bayeux Tapestry!) that all could join in with. In effect, you can make this as simple or as complex as you wish. All you need to remember is that you will use more materials than you think (there will be many screwed-up balls of paper and 'final attempts'!).

As a group, decide what form the event will take. It could be a group activity (i.e. all try to represent the same item – like an art class – but in different materials). It could be an individual activity, where each person does their own creative thing. Or it could be a mixture of both. Whichever you choose, you need to plan carefully. If you have an art teacher (or a junior school teacher who teaches art) in the church, you may want to encourage them to run the afternoon for you. This will reduce your stress, and make the event more enjoyable for everyone else!

The next thing to decide is where the event will take place. You could go for a walk and paint an outside scene, but if the event is to take place indoors, you need to be somewhere where the carpets and wallpaper do not matter – and where the room can be cleaned easily! You might even be able to hire a school classroom designed for this purpose.

You may want to offer soft drinks during the afternoon, so be aware that this will also need planning. Of course, if you are using food (fruit, etc.) to paint or represent, you can then have great fun eating it afterwards!

Finally, if you want a focus for the afternoon, display your efforts in the church, or get your leader to act as judge and award a prize.

GUESTS

This is a great event to invite both young and old to, and is particularly appropriate for families. Mums and dads will enjoy 'playing' and there will be quite a lot of inter-generational competition! It will also be interesting to see if there are any budding Picassos in your church or cell group!

COST

The cost of this afternoon will depend upon the sort of materials you use. Most art materials are very expensive, so go for cheap poster paints and a paper that works with watercolours. Collage can be very cheap because you can use everyday scraps from magazines, bits of rag, etc. Obviously the drinks may cost you a little, but hopefully not very much.

You could, if you wish, recoup some of these costs by making a small charge for attendance. It will depend on how much you spend and whether or not you feel comfortable about charging.

VARIATIONS

You can try different aspects of art. For instance:

- A photographic afternoon – you may be able to find some keen amateurs in your church willing to help, or a local photography shop willing to sponsor an afternoon's lesson. This will involve some cost to the participants for developing, etc.
- Mural or collage painting.
- Banner creation. (If they are good, you could use them in church.)
- Christmas card making.

You may find some very creative talents in your group that you were previously unaware of. Find them, encourage them and use them!

2 Barbecue

PLANNING

The barbecue is probably the easiest and most popular out-reach event. Planning is minimal: all you really have to do is arrange a day, plan the food and drink, and pray for good weather! Like the ubiquitous cheese and wine evening, you can 'spice up' the day by introducing different themes or moods (see below). The great advantage of this event is that it can be either a daytime or an evening event and people of all ages can attend and enjoy. If your aim is to get to know families well, this is the event for you. However, critical to its success is having a big enough barbecue and a big enough garden. Also, ensure that there are enough chairs for the number of people you will have.

GUESTS

Provided your garden is big enough, you can invite as many people as you like. In fact all the members of your group can invite someone, as families, older couples and single people all mingle well at a barbecue. This event is ideal for disabled people, as well as the elderly.

COST

The cost of a barbecue is like the proverbial length of string, but if each member of your group can bring some food or drink, then the cost should be minimal. You will probably find that guests like to bring something, as it seems to be part of the culture of the barbecue.

VARIATIONS

To vary the event, and to stop it from being too much the same as every other barbecue you have ever been to, try:

- Garden games (e.g. swingball, garden cricket, Frisbee).

- A paddling pool, if there are young families. Enjoy watching the children get themselves, and you, wet!

- Theme barbecues – Mexican, all sausage (there is an infinite variety these days) or Australian (get the steaks out!) can all be good fun, especially if you get the music to fit.

- All-fish barbecues – fish are great on the barbecue and it's good fun guessing which fish you've just eaten.

OUR EXPERIENCE

By using barbecues as a social activity throughout the Alpha weeks (that is, extra social activities) we have found that we get to know the attendees better, and we get to meet their families earlier, which invariably means that we have a new pool to draw from for the next Alpha. By doing this, we have often held barbecues with as many as 15 to 20 non-Christians or church attendees. We have also found that it works extremely well for our cell groups. Attendance has been high and the contacts longer lasting.

3 Barn Dance

PLANNING

Barn dances are about fun and activity, and while dancing to albums can be fun, it is much better to use a live band with a true caller. The planning for this session is based around this concept.

Planning a barn dance starts with the date, and this will be determined by the availability of the band, the venue and your groups (and of these the first two are the most important). You will be able to find a good band through your local music stores, adverts in the press and by asking around (try your local library for more information, or local Country & Western or line dancing clubs). If in doubt about the skills and prowess of the band you are thinking about, ask for references. The band should not mind, and it could save you some embarrassment later! Once the band and the venue are booked, you can then go ahead with the remainder of the planning.

Next, decide what sort of food and drink you intend to offer. Try things like sausage and beans if you want a Western night; a ploughman's-style platter for a Country feel; cheese and wine for the more unadventurous; a barbecue for the ambitious; jacket potato and fillings for the well planned!

Having decided on food and drink, decide how much you would like to charge your guests. I would suggest that £5 is about the limit.

Advertise through your local press, posters and invitation

cards about six weeks prior to the event. Sell tickets in advance, as this will give you a feel for how many people will turn out. You will need between 75 and 100 people to make this a successful event, so your planning needs to take this into consideration.

In the final week or two before the event, delegate the food and drink preparation to a number of people. During the final week, check that your volunteers are actually doing what they agreed to do and arrange the time they will arrive with their offerings. Check again on the day. It is amazing how many people 'didn't realize that you meant *this* Saturday' or have had events that have delayed them or stopped them! Checking on the day allows you the opportunity to sort out the problem.

During the preceding weeks you should call the band again to make sure that you clearly understand their needs and wants, including the following:

- What time will they need access on the day?

- What time will they leave?

- What will be the *total* cost of the band (including PA, etc.)?

- What PA will they bring and what will you need to provide?

- How long will they perform and how many sessions will they provide (i.e. will there be breaks)?

- Do you need to provide food for them before or during the event?

- How much help will they need in unloading and loading their equipment?

- Will they be bringing their own guests (spouses, etc.)?

Asking these sorts of questions will avoid misunderstandings and panic! It will also help you in shaping your planning for the day itself.

Turning to the day, you should plan to be at the venue at least two hours before the event. This is to make sure that you are there for the band and the arrival of the food (although if this is a cold buffet you could arrange for it to arrive earlier in the day, which will help you later on). If you are very ambitious and do not mind clearing up afterwards, you could arrange to have some hay bales brought in to give that authentic feel. If not, make sure that there are some chairs for people to sit on during dances and for when they are eating. Remember, not everyone has your energy or willingness to stand around for ever.

Appoint someone to be the 'master of ceremonies' during the event to ensure that the evening goes according to plan. You might want to have two distinct parts to the evening, separated by an interval for food. This gives people time to rest and recuperate.

Finally, barn dancing is a participatory event, so make sure that there are dances for all ages and abilities. Inevitably some people will be very good, but the vast majority will be fairly average, which means that you can include both children and elderly people. Your caller should be able to judge the pace of the evening to ensure that all can join in.

Make sure that you have enough people available at the end of the event to help you pack up quickly and efficiently.

GUESTS

Invite anyone and everyone. Young and old alike will enjoy a good barn dance. It is a very sociable event, so invite as many people as possible. This means that it is not a small cell-group event, but an excellent whole-church event. Advertise it as such and you will find that church members will invite many people you will not have come across, without worrying about the cringe factor.

COST

Cost will be determined by your decision over whether to use a band or not. A good band should cost between £100 and £300, depending on how many members there are. For this you should get about two and a half hours' playing time and fun. If you have your own church hall, there will be no cost for hall hire. If not, it is possible to pay as little as £100 for the night. Your food and drink should cost very little because it is being provided by your volunteers. The total cost should be between £300 and £400, meaning that if you can get 100 guests, you will be well within your £5 per head ticket price. Allow a little for children, as this will encourage families to attend – say £3.50 per child under 16.

VARIATIONS

As mentioned above, varying the food can add variety to the standard barn dance:

• Western: sausage and beans.

• Barbecue.

• Country: ploughman's.

You could also try a Scottish or Irish ceilidh: the idea of including dancing, story-telling and singing could make for a particularly enjoyable event, but this needs planning well with the help of an expert. An event like this could bring in a very different sort of guest and would be a very enjoyable night.

FOLLOW-UP

Another family activity, such as a barbecue or picnic, would be well received and enjoyed by all. During the event, an invitation to an Alpha course would be appropriate, though only in a low-key way.

OUR EXPERIENCE

The barn dance is a very enjoyable and inclusive event. We have developed many good contacts through this event, and we have followed up the event with other activities. We have used the barn dance as the centrepiece of our church cell-group harvest week. The planning was left to a small planning committee based around a cell group or group of cells, and the event was advertised church-wide.

4 Beauty Makeover

PLANNING

You will need to plan a date and venue (small groups will be more comfortable in a home, larger groups in a suitable venue that is still small enough to make it feel warm and intimate), and invite speakers and demonstrators. Samples will need to be acquired and advice sought.

Having said that, there are some 'easy' alternatives. For example, this is an ideal event to invite some local businesses to participate in. There will be some hairdressers and beauticians who are peripatetic (i.e. work by home visiting) and would be delighted to be able to advertise their business to a group of interested ladies. Inevitably they will bring their own samples, so the cost to you could be very little. Some small clothing stores may be willing to bring samples for you to look at and discuss. If you plan early enough, you will be able to find quite a few such businesses.

If you want to do this by yourself or keep it within your group, it is important to be sure you know what you are talking about as a little knowledge is a dangerous thing. In addition, you will need to bring your own samples, so the cost will start to rise significantly.

Decide what food and drinks to provide throughout the evening, and ask your group(s) to bring what you need.

In briefing your speakers, make sure that plenty of time is allowed for questions and chatting, as this is an essential part of the evening. In addition, ask your speakers to be conscious of cost to their hearers, as it will be a temptation to use only the best materials, and these could be out of your guests' income reach. Finally, stress the need to make this a demonstration and hands-on approach because this will make the evening much more enjoyable.

GUESTS

While there will be many men who would love to attend this event, it may be more appropriate to make it a girls only night! Try to make this a cross-generational event where possible, as this allows people to mix with other age groups. Many of the older ladies will have invaluable advice to offer.

COST

If your invited speakers and demonstrators are willing to speak for free on the basis that they may pick up some business, then the cost will really only be the food and drink that you as a group lay on.

VARIATIONS

You could make this a morning event, especially if, as a church, you either have your own morning parents and toddlers group or your church building hosts one. Alternatively, you could make this an event for young women (16–20), in which case make sure you are up to date on the latest new looks!

FOLLOW-UP

A great follow-up to this evening is to host a fashion show. This could be planned during the beauty evening and will allow your guests to show off what they have learned. It will also allow the more adventurous to try their hand at something very different to see what they look and feel like! Alternatively, you could try some of the more traditional party plan style activities.

OUR EXPERIENCE

One of our house groups tried this as a ladies' beauty night and had a great time. The venue for the evening was a local shop where the owners were able to talk about their business. On the whole this was well received because the perception was that the demonstrator was a professional and could give good advice.

The evening was well planned and executed, and the non-Christian guests were made to feel very welcome. All the ladies who attended were looking forward to the next one! We felt, though, that we needed to be a little more focused, perhaps choosing one aspect of make-up or fashion, such as colour co-ordination.

5 Bonfire Night

PLANNING

The planning of this event will depend upon whether you put on your own event or attend an organized display. Organizing your own bonfire can be great fun . . . but. And it is a big but. Safety has become a big issue over the last few years. When I was a child, we all had our own bonfires and fireworks. These days very few people have their own bonfire night, mainly due to the safety aspect. Therefore, only host your own bonfire if you are sure you have enough space and that the utmost care will be taken by anyone handling fireworks. It is important to have safety aids at hand, such as sand, water and a first aid kit.

Assuming that you have plenty of room and that you have taken on board the need for safety and protection, planning your own bonfire and fireworks party is great fun. Children will enjoy helping to put the bonfire together – collecting, dragging and stacking. They will also enjoy making a Guy Fawkes (best not put a mask of your mother-in-law or pastor on it though) and this all adds to the fun of the night.

On the night itself, don't light the bonfire too early. Wait until everyone has arrived. *And never use petrol or other lighter fluid to light it!* Also, make sure that you keep every-one as far back as possible, as accidents can and do happen (bonfire night is one of the most high-risk nights of the year).

Ask your friends to bring their own fireworks if you wish (it is cheaper for you that way!). These should be stored in a metal container with a lid (which stays on). Never let children light fireworks, and follow the instructions very carefully. Do not return to lit fireworks to see why they have not gone off.

Prior to the night, decide what food and drink you will provide. Warm food, such as soup, a barbecue and/or baked potatoes, always goes down well.

If you decide to go to an organized event, book your tickets early. The cost of a ticket includes food and drinks at some venues, but not necessarily so. Your local fire officer will be able to tell you which are the approved events, and your friends will have a good idea which have the best fireworks. Parking might be a problem at the larger events, so be prepared for a long walk.

GUESTS

Most of us can remember the magic of bonfire night. It forms part of our childhood. It is a family event so ask your friends and relatives.

COST

Cost will depend upon which route you take. Your own event will include the cost of fireworks, food and drink. If each family brings their own, the cost will be greatly reduced. Going to organized events can cost as much as £5 each.

VARIATIONS

You could consider making this a fancy dress event. Why not try a bonfire night in the summer or early spring, when there's lots of garden rubbish to burn? It's something a little different to have fireworks in March, although they may be harder to get hold of.

OUR EXPERIENCE

We often attend a local event that is very family orientated and not that big or expensive. This means that we have been able to invite our neighbours to come with us, and we have enjoyed good company through the evening. Again, we have mixed our Christian and non-Christian friends to good effect.

We have also had our own garden bonfire/firework party with our neighbours (we do have an 80-foot garden!), which has been great fun. It has been a good way to get to know our neighbours and the cost has been minimal.

6 Book Party

PLANNING

This particular event is actually very easy to organize and host. First of all, you simply need to find someone who plans and hosts parties for others, Dorling Kindersley are particularly good at booking parties, and will provide all you need for the event. There are other book party people, and a quick check in your local *Yellow Pages* may help.

Once you have agreed the date with your party organizer, the rest is easy. A good organizer will give you party invites for your friends, and all you have to do is get people along.

The emphasis of this event is not on a full-scale evangelistic preach, but on building friendship, having fun and introducing your non-Christian friends to your Christian friends – although you may want to give all your guests an Alpha leaflet or church leaflet.

In terms of planning, your organizer will advise you on whether to have food or drinks, and it's wise to follow their advice as they are the professionals!

GUESTS

Invite a cross-section of people: Christians and non-Christians, old and young. Be aware that some of your guests may not be able to spend as much as others, so be sensitive but not protective.

41

COST

The only cost you should have is your food and drinks. Most party plan companies offer incentives to the host, so you may actually end up in credit. Of course, if you choose to buy anything, then the cost will rise, but that is your call!

VARIATIONS

You could try all sorts of variations – the list of companies that have party plans is increasing:

- Tupperware/Betterware.
- Clothing.
- Food.
- Music.

Try approaching your local Christian bookshop. They have a great variety of good stock that could form part of a party plan. They will be able to come and talk about their books, music, cards and gifts. If you explain that the idea is low-key friendship evangelism, they will be able to promote books about the family, good biographies, issues books and children's books. There is also plenty of good Christian music with a low cringe factor! If you have never tried such an event, the excellent materials now available will surprise you.

Christmas is a great time to think of these ideas as people are always looking for that special gift.

OUR EXPERIENCE

Our groups have hosted such parties in the past, and a number of women in particular have enjoyed actually becoming party planners. It is ideal for getting into non-Christian homes, and for inviting people to something that they will recognize and enjoy. We have had some very good contacts from these events, which have finally resulted in new believers being added to the church.

7 Business Visit

A trip to a local business for a behind-the-scenes look works on the basis of curiosity. In most towns and cities there are some very interesting businesses that can offer a fascinating insight into a world of which most people are unaware.

PLANNING

An event like this is easier to arrange if you have a good contact in the business; approaching it from cold can be hard work. In our area we have several very interesting businesses, such as a recording studio and a cider-making plant. If you struggle to find anything of interest, you may have a local sports team that you can visit (soccer stadiums are excellent for this).

In the first instance, write to the company concerned to ask whether you can bring a group of interested local people for a visit. If the company is at all interested in the local community, it is likely to agree. Make sure that there are enough interested people wishing to visit to make it worthwhile to the company. You may need to visit the company beforehand to check that there is enough to hold your group's interest.

On the visit itself, you may need to go round in smaller groups to get the best benefit from the trip. If you strike lucky, there will not be a charge – and there may even be some 'freebies' on offer. If not, you may need to make a charge. Sometimes the company already does visitor tours

(Cadbury's, Old Trafford, for example), and these trips are straightforward in terms of planning and costs.

Once a date has been agreed and an agenda set (if necessary), you can go ahead with publicizing the event.

GUESTS

In reality only those who are interested will bother coming out. For example, visiting a local recording studio will be of great interest to anyone who has more than a passing interest in the music industry – they will be fascinated to see how an album is really made.

COST

The trip could be free, but if it is to an established tourist venue, then the cost could be between £5 and £10 per head. You must cut your cloth according to your willingness to pay.

VARIATIONS

Graphic designers, local newspapers and large companies with interesting products are all excellent places to visit.

OUR EXPERIENCE

Having taken groups of sales people around a recording studio, I began to realize the interest that could be created by such a trip. In fact, it can be hard getting people out of an interesting business. It has opened up some fascinating conversations and questions – often the most stupid-sounding question has created the best conversations.

8 Car Treasure Hunt

PLANNING

This event requires a number of cars careering around the locality trying to find clues while keeping up with each other. Clearly there is a huge potential for disaster – lost cars, lost clues, to name but two! The success of this event lies in the planning.

About six weeks before the event, plan the route you wish the cars to take. Try to make it interesting and take people to places they are unlikely to go to under normal circumstances. Try to include local highlights – as well as lowlights! The route should really be about 10 to 15 miles at most. This allows for about 10 clues, but you should allow an average of 1.5 miles per clue. Having planned the route, you then need to drive around to look for ideas. It helps to have two of you setting the clues. They should not be too obvious (you need to make the drivers stop to look for clues), nor should they be too hard (how many *Mastermind* winners do you have in your church?). Be very careful – the clues will say more about you than you think!

In setting the clues, be as accurate as possible. The hunters will try to claim all sorts of answers if you are not very careful! You might like to consider the following:

- Telephone box numbers.

- Fire hydrant numbers.

- Birth/death dates or names in cemeteries.

- Price of fuel in a petrol station or of goods in a shop window.

- Names on park benches or plaques, etc.

- Signposts (e.g. What are the total miles on the signpost on the junction of . . . ?).

- Poster information.

- Menu costs (e.g. How much will a 24 and a 36 with fried rice cost at the . . . ?).

- Curiosities (e.g. What is commemorated at . . . ?).

- Opening hours.

Above all, try to be off-beat or challenging with about half of the clues. It will make people think and they will enjoy the evening better.

Once the initial planning is complete, type up the clues so that they are clear. Print the course rules clearly on the sheet, including sticking to speed limits and driving carefully, and how points are awarded.

Several days before the event, ask a friend to follow the course. This will ensure that (a) all the clues are still there; (b) you have a rough estimation of the time it will take (you can omit some clues if it takes too long); and (c) the clues are all understandable. Once you know the course time, you will then also be able to deduct points if the drivers are too fast. The temptation to break the speed limit or cut corners is too strong for some people – especially reps and other professional drivers!

Make sure that the route takes the guests to a venue, be that someone's home, a church hall or a restaurant, and ensure that food and drink are available. Remember that as some are driving alcohol is not a smart idea!

Finally, there must be a prize for first, and a wooden

spoon for last. As there will be several people in each car, several prizes will be required.

Caution: It might be a good idea to check with your local constabulary that they do not mind you organizing the event. Also check any insurance questions.

GUESTS

Plan to have at least three people in each car as they can then take turns in answering the clues and have a good laugh at the same time. Such events build friendships quickly and the groups are small enough for everyone to join in. People of all ages can join in, and this is an ideal activity for including family units. In this case, be prepared to split them up so that they mingle with other people. If someone brings a friend, it is important that they stay together for the event.

COST

Apart from fuel, the cost to the guests should be minimal, unless you charge for food. I would suggest a finger buffet if you are putting the food on, or a pizza house if you go to a restaurant. The prizes should be fun but relevant (e.g. character in-car 'smellies' or miniature Corgi cars, etc.) and therefore inexpensive.

VARIATIONS

This event does not depend on the weather, unless it is snowing or foggy. Plan to do this event in the spring, summer or autumn when the days are longer (early evening or a weekend is an ideal time to do a car treasure hunt). If there is interest, you could do a treasure hunt on foot. This can be just as much fun, provided the weather holds.

FOLLOW-UP

The sort of person who has enjoyed this event is likely to enjoy other similar events, such as quiz nights or Trivial Pursuit. During the food at the end, ask around to see what other events are of interest, and pursue them quickly.

OUR EXPERIENCE

All the people who took part in both the car and on-foot hunts had a great time. We tagged a meal onto one and a barbecue onto the other. Food was an important reason for people coming along. We had several non-Christian guests on both and were able to follow up at a later stage, though rather loosely in our case.

9 Car-Washing in Car Parks

PLANNING

The most obvious place to do this activity is where the most cars are! On Saturday mornings this would be the local supermarket car park. However, bear in mind that most supermarkets have a petrol station with a car wash attached, and they may not want to lose income in this way. This being the case, you may want to attach yourself to a local shopping area (for example a small terrace of popular shops) or a small shopping mall where this would not be a problem. Choose the car park you wish to work in, and then seek permission from the manager of the super-market or shopping mall, and find out about access to hot water.

You need to have a reason other than 'evangelism', so I would strongly advise choosing a charity to work with. This could be local (the local mayor's charity is always a good one to choose) or an internationally well-known charity (e.g. TEAR Fund). However, there may be other good charities you wish to associate with for a number of reasons. Decide how much you will charge for each car (probably no more than £1).

Decide how many people you will need. I would suggest four teams of four people, 16 in all. This way each team has someone for each side, front and back! Each person will need a bucket, warm water (available throughout the day), suit-able cleaning materials and a sponge. If each person were to bring the basic materials from home, that would mean you would only have to supply water and suitable cleaning chemicals.

I would also suggest having a couple of other people to help organize the event on the day. You will need to have someone at the entrance of the car park asking each driver if they want their car cleaned. If they do, they should be given a ticket (a cloakroom ticket would be fine) and directed to a special area of the car park. This should have been pre-agreed with the site manager and should be close enough for your customers not to have to walk too far with heavy bags or trolleys. A second person needs to be on hand to welcome the drivers back to their cars, and charge them for a job well done!

Plan to hold another event in your church shortly after the car-washing and advertise the fact on leaflets ready for distribution to your 'customers'. This could be a special service, or the visit of a well-known name (sporting heroes or a big concert are great follow-up ideas). Alternatively, it could be a big church barbecue or bonfire (depending on the time of year). Whatever it is, it needs to be creative and interesting so that it captures people's imagination.

This sort of event is ideal for a young people's group (youth group, Boys' Brigade, etc.) or for a couple of cell groups. But it could also be a family activity, or run by older people who have time on their hands. In fact there are no limits to who you could ask along to help, except that they will need to have some common sense so that you do not damage someone else's pride and joy!

COST

There really should not be any cost beyond the liquid cleaning agents needed, so this is a great event for those with small budgets.

VARIATIONS

Rather than washing the whole car, you could try wind-screen-washing at a local petrol station. This is obviously quicker and could be more effective, as you can chat with the people still in the car as well as give them leaflets. If you do use this option, you may need to accept that you are offering your services free of charge, as you cannot insist that people pay you for such a small service!

10 Celebration Meal

PLANNING

Most churches have set-piece occasions centred on some form of baptism, thanksgiving or confirmation. As these are well attended by family and friends who want to support the person involved, they are ideal opportunities for your cell group to put on a good event for them. You need to agree quite what that could entail, but the meal either before or after is fairly easy to arrange.

A meal beforehand could take the form of a breakfast (assuming that most such services are in the morning). It does not have to be that special – the fact that you are willing to host a meal will be impressive enough. If you have the facilities and manpower, a cooked breakfast will extend you, but will be good fun. If you have room, a 'silver service' waiter/waitress format is very impressive. If you don't have the facilities, the room or the manpower, a continental breakfast is very easy and not that expensive. See below for the sort of foods that work well.

If you decide on an after-service meal, this can take the simple form of a picnic or barbecue, both of which are easy to arrange. If you like the idea of a more formal setting, you can arrange an indoor finger buffet, or go the whole distance and host a formal waiter/waitress attended meal.

Decide which is the best option for you, bearing in mind that it is important to ensure that all your cell group members agree to play their part. Otherwise you will end up as the chief cook and bottle-washer!

GUESTS

The guests will mostly be the friends and family of the person being baptized, confirmed or whatever. However, this is also an excellent opportunity to invite your own friends to the service, as the sermon should be quite evangelistic.

COST

The cost will depend wholly on the sort of arrangement you make. The after-church picnic is cheap, the barbecue not quite as cheap, and the sit-down meal could be very expensive. However, you do need to keep the costs as low as possible so that your group does not get financially embarrassed.

VARIATIONS

If you have other set-piece services, you should make every opportunity to use a meal to invite your friends to stay longer. It is in fact the opportunity to introduce the Alpha course, as this too revolves around a sit-down meal.

FOLLOW-UP

Alpha is an obvious follow-up to this meal as it is close to it in style and content. Try to keep in contact with the people who come to such services. The easiest way is to give each visitor a welcome pack and ask them to fill in a simple form with their name and address. This enables you to write to them in the following week, thanking them for attending and offering the Alpha course or other opportunities to meet. Most people appreciate this sort of letter as it shows an interest in them and says that they were noticed and are welcome to return.

OUR EXPERIENCE

We have found non-Christians attending baptisms and other more formal occasions to be very open to staying for a meal. In fact most of them are 'blown away' by the generosity of the church. We find them to be open, chatty and willing to engage in deeper conversation as a result. We have always been pleased with the results of the effort, and would heartily recommend the concept to you. One word of caution though. Most people's image of the church meal is dry stale sandwiches, strong tea and home-made cakes. Be extravagant and professional about the meal, and the results will be even better.

11 Cheese and Wine Evening

PLANNING

By far and away the most popular event put on by churches, the cheese and wine party is easy to organize but in danger of being tired and boring. Good planning will help to avert these dangers and will keep the interest of your group and guests. Planning need only be two to three weeks before the event, and this is for invitations to be sent out and followed up. Plan the food carefully so that not everyone brings the same thing. You might like to try a country theme (e.g. French cheese and wine) or cheeses that are unusual (see below). Vary the food and wine (use Indian breads or Italian-style salads, etc.) to create interest. Planning early will help you keep on track with what you need to do.

GUESTS

Anyone and everyone! Cheese and wine evenings can be enjoyed by all. Make sure that there are sufficient non-Christian guests as people can easily feel intimidated by a large group of people who already know each other. Also, make sure that your Christian guests are circulating and not just chatting to each other. Having brought someone along, don't waste the time by ignoring him or her!

COST

Cost is variable, depending on how much you want to push the boat out. Of course, you could reduce costs by asking everyone to bring their own bottle of wine or drink.

VARIATIONS

Try these for a different style of evening:

- A non-alcoholic wine evening – there are some great non- and low-alcoholic wines on the market at present.

- All French cheeses, wine and music evening.

- Sheep's or goat's cheese evening.

- Fondue evening (better for smaller, intimate groups).

- Pre-prepared warm cheese salad evening.

- Ploughman's evening.

- Cheese in different dishes (e.g. grand nachos, Welsh rarebit, deep-fried breaded cheese).

By being creative, you can change an old formula into an interesting evening. Remember, the more unique the evening, the more you will have to plan.

FOLLOW-UP

This is an ideal evening in which to hand out leaflets to guests – the church leaflet, an Alpha course leaflet or a concert/event leaflet. This allows guests to read at their own leisure.

OUR EXPERIENCE

We have found that all sorts of people have responded to an invitation to a cheese and wine evening, but that they are better as either a follow-up to other events or a first introduction to the group. As this event is so easy to put on, most of our groups have done so, with varying degrees of success. We have used literature at the end of the event in a non-threatening way, and have held evenings without literature. Most have been successful in terms of meeting new friends and building on existing relationships.

12 Christmas Carol Service

Most churches are experts at Christmas carol services. I cannot presume to teach my grandmother to suck eggs, so the basis of this chapter is not to help you organize a Christmas carol service, but to ask you to look at some alternatives that will draw people into your church.

At the heart of the Christmas carol service is the proclamation of the birth of the Saviour. It is also high on most people's agenda as one of the three church services they will attend in one year (barring christenings, weddings and funerals). Therefore, we need to work out how we can attract as many people as possible into our churches at that time.

Why not approach your local schools to see what they are doing this year? Many of them will hold a carol service to which parents are invited. This is nice if the parents are not working or can take time off work. Unfortunately, many parents do work and cannot take time off to see little Johnny sing his heart out. This is disappointing for the parent and child! In addition, many schools have space problems when it comes to seating 200-plus children, teachers and parents. So why not invite them to hold their carol service twice: once at school during school time and once on a Sunday afternoon in your church? You could then combine it with your own carol service. You will find that many schools will be delighted to work with you (especially if some or all of the collection was given to the school fund!). The net result could mean that your church is packed out for the first time in years with non-Christians: children, parents, teachers and grannies!

PLANNING

In terms of planning, you need to talk to schools around September time to give them opportunity to talk through the implications and their own planning. Be clear that you would like there to be a ten-minute talk about the meaning of Christmas, but if you say ten minutes, make sure it doesn't become 15!

As part of your planning, decide what information you would like to give your guests and how to give it to them. For example, you could give Alpha leaflets or information about your own services. You should have a church leaflet that states your basic beliefs and a short but punchy gospel message. Give that away.

Also, you need to think about food and drink. Perhaps you could have some warm mince pies available or some good Christmas snacks (see Delia Smith for help!) after the service with tea and coffee, or a non-alcoholic, warm, spicy mulled wine.

Finally, back to your ten-minute talk. Make it funny, informative, punchy and gospel-orientated. Take the opportunity that is there, but not in the form of a 50-minute preach. Remember, where there are parents and school children, there will also be lots of other even smaller children. Moreover, there is a further added benefit to you as a church. If you plan this well and make a good job, most schools will be willing to welcome you into their school for assemblies. The pay off for being sensible can be huge!

GUESTS

These will be invited by the school itself: parents, teachers and relatives. You should also open it up to your own church. Don't see this as the school hiring your building for an event. This is about partnership between the school and your church, and your congregation should be encouraged to see this as an excellent opportunity.

COST

If you are having food and drink as described, this should be your only cost. Keep it simple but excellent.

VARIATIONS

If you are ready to try other such events, various school and church festivals lend themselves to this opportunity:

- Easter.
- Harvest.
- End of year thanksgiving.
- School concerts.

FOLLOW-UP

If you are organized, you could arrange one of your other events to happen shortly afterwards. This means that your congregation can meet their friends in church (I am assuming here that your congregation have non-Christian friends at the service either through the school or as guests of the church) and invite them to another event shortly after – preferably within the next two weeks. You could also invite them to your Alpha supper so that they can find out more about the life and death of the baby they have just celebrated.

Whatever you do, make sure that this service is not in a void or a vacuum and simply another service. Use it to your best advantage with careful planning of other events around it.

OUR EXPERIENCE

We invited one of our local schools to help us with a Sunday afternoon carol service. The result was that we had over 300 parents/friends/family members in church, coming to hear little Johnny and hearing the gospel. We used it as an invitation to Alpha and other gospel-aimed meetings, as well as promoting our Saturday morning Kids Club (which has found a considerable increase in numbers after such a service).

There is one other brief comment I would like to make. The church in this country has, in reality, organized Christmas for itself, not for the community at large. Beginning to work with the local community as outlined above may well mean that you have to organize your church Christmas around their needs, not yours. Be aware that the traditional people in your church may not appreciate this move, as the outside world often moves to the beat of a different drum, and the timing might not be the same! It is an ideal time to reach out to others, but there may be some costs that you had not thought about.

13 Christmas Gift-Wrapping

The idea here is to offer a gift-wrapping service in the town centre during the Christmas season.

PLANNING

Saturdays are a good day to offer this service as the town centre will be heaving on the four Saturdays prior to Christmas. Regrettably, the same is true for the four Sundays prior to Christmas. Discuss among yourselves whether or not to offer the service on both days (a case for the church going to the people?). If you do decide to do this, you may even want to host a service in the town centre, but more planning is needed for this. As most churches should be good at organizing open-air-style services, I will concentrate on the original idea, assuming a Saturday-only policy.

First, decide where to have your gift-wrapping station. It should be in a busy area, but not too much in the way of the vast number of shoppers who could see you as a nuisance. Secondly, try to ensure that you are indoors if possible – the local indoor market or shopping mall would be excellent. Thirdly, if you are indoors (a must if it is cold and wet) you will need the permission of the centre management – or risk being moved on!

Having chosen your site well, plan what you will need: at least one large table (depending on how many of you there are), a pair of scissors each, sellotape and gift-wrap. Ideally you will have several sorts of wrapping paper so that your 'clients' may choose the one they prefer. If you want to go the extra mile, you could offer matching gift tags that your 'clients' can write on while you wrap (it saves forgetting which present is for which person later on!).

Finally, you need to have enough people to carry the day. I would suggest several teams of, say, four people: three people to wrap, one to chat to people. If you start at 10.00 am and work through until 4.00 pm, you will need three teams to do two hours each, a total of twelve people. If you have enough people, you could do one Saturday each – a total of 48 people! However, you may want to arrange this in a different way. This is down to you, but try to spread it across as many people as possible.

There are some other important matters to take care of on the planning side. First of all, you need to ensure that you have a concert or carol service that you can invite people to during the Christmas period. This being the case, give a pre-printed leaflet to every client advertising the events you have planned. One thing leads to another! I would also suggest that you have some overt evangelistic materials available – maybe Alpha leaflets or personal tracts – that can be given away. People are going to be curious, so be prepared to offer a full range of leaflets. Also, if you have a church banner, use it to advertise your church and activities.

Consider using music as a means of getting people's attention – loud Christmas music is best suited – but check beforehand whether you need permission to play music in a public place in your town. Further, if you are in your local shopping mall, you may want to put leaflets in all the stores in the mall so that your services are advertised.

Finally, you may want to offer drinks and pies (mince pies and warm mulled wine will go down a treat) to entice people to stay and chat.

COST

There will be the cost of the wrapping paper, gift tags and sellotape, but you might get a local card shop to underwrite some of these things, or at least sell them cheaply – especially if you have your stand outside their store and advertise the fact that they are sponsoring the stand. If you choose to have food and drinks, there will be some cost involved here too. Thus, you should be prepared for costs of up to about £100 per day if you choose to go ahead, although you could offset this by charging people per parcel, or by asking them for a voluntary payment.

Consider choosing a local charity and asking your clients to make a voluntary contribution to the cause. If you choose the local mayor's charity, he or she may actually come and publicize your stand, which would be great for publicity in the local newspapers for all involved! (This would give your local card shop more reason for offering the gift-wrap free or cheaply!)

VARIATIONS

It is difficult to see other times of the year when this sort of activity would be suitable, but the Saturday prior to Mother's Day could work in the busy towns and cities.

14 Christmas in June

This is a Christmas party with a difference because it can be held at any time of the year – especially in the summer. After all, the Australians have all the fun of having a Christmas barbecue in the sun, so why can't we?

PLANNING

Having agreed to the date (perhaps the 25th of a month), you need to retrieve your Christmas decorations from the loft and put them up. Christmas trees will be hard to find in June, but you could use an artificial tree with its own decorations.

Christmas food is now easy to find in supermarkets at any time of the year. If you are having traditional Christmas fayre, then get your turkey, peel the spuds and have yourself a merry, merry Christmas. Alternatively, you could go for the Christmas barbecue, or try a Christmas dish from another country (there are some excellent cookery books available that give such recipes). For the party, you could have lots of Christmas-type nibbles (again, see the Christmas party books).

For drinks, mulled wine and non-alcoholic punches are easy to put together.

You will need to dig out your Christmas music too. As it is a party, find a fun album and play it loud and long. After all, shouldn't we celebrate the birth of our Saviour all year round?

One small point: Christmas is not Christmas without gifts, so everyone who comes should bring a useless but fun gift costing less than £3. Put them into the middle of the floor, and hand them out to anyone and everyone. It will help bring a smile in the middle of a rainy summer!

Also, get out your stock of Christmas games. Charades and other perennials will add to the feeling that Christmas really is here. Don't be afraid to use them – your guests will be half-expecting them. Again, there are some great little books with Christmas party games for the over-fives. And why not have a Father Christmas? He could hand out your gifts. You can get costumes from a local fancy dress shop (see your *Yellow Pages*).

Finally, you need to wear some festive clothing. You could ask people to wear fancy dress, or follow a colour code: men in red, women in green.

GUESTS

As this will be an unusual party, it might be a good idea to explain to your neighbours what you are doing – so why not invite them? If they know you are a Christian, they probably already think that you are from the planet Zorg, so why not help cement that view? As to other guests, your cell group should invite people who would enjoy Christmas in the summer (this presupposes a group of people with friends who enjoy the bizarre). Invite people who know how to enjoy themselves. In addition, children enjoy a great Christmas party, so make it a family affair.

Finally, most people enjoy Christmas from about the 1st September (when the shops start stocking up on Christmas crackers, etc.) to the end of October. By the 25th December they are waiting for it to finish so that they can carry on with their lives. Having Christmas early means that they can enjoy a one-off party and have fun.

COST

Cost will depend on how far you go. Apart from the food and drink (and your useless but fun £3 gift), try to keep the costs as low as possible. By being creative (your cell group can bring parts of the food) and asking everyone to bring a drink, you can keep the cost low. Bringing in caterers will obviously increase costs significantly.

VARIATIONS

There are some other popular times of the year that you could move temporarily – bonfire night, Easter and Valentine's Day are good examples. Why not host a late Millennium party?

15 Colour Evening

PLANNING

The overall aim of this event is to have a theme night based on colour. For example, if the colour is red, then the clothes you wear, the drinks you consume and the food you eat all need to be different shades of red. Remember that some colours will be easier than others, so your planning should allow time to think about the options available to you. For example, what will be available to you if you choose purple? Of course, if you choose the right colours, the music can be blended in with the theme. Band names will help, for example Simply Red, Red Hot Chilli Peppers (which also works well with a great chilli night) and Pink Floyd. (Black Sabbath might not be that appropriate, though, so be careful!)

A colour evening will need about six weeks to plan: one week to agree the idea and the date, and five weeks to invite your guests.

GUESTS

Anyone who likes a little fun will enjoy this event. So will those who are a little more adventurous with their food. Eating familiar food in a different colour can be off-putting for some people, so you need to be clear with your guests about what the evening will entail.

COST

Cost should be minimal, as most people have many different colours in their wardrobes. Watch the 60s and 70s styles come out if you choose the right colour! Most foods can be dyed with the right colour (such edible food dyes are available at your local supermarkets), as can most drinks. As you will expect your group to bring food selections, there is not much cost here. You can buy the relevant colour balloons and party ware (e.g. napkins and plates, etc.) at pretty low cost, so overall you should not expect to spend that much.

VARIATIONS

Colour options are the main variations open to you, though you could do two colours together, say red and green (which could confuse those who are colour blind). Some foods that are easily dyed are:

- Rice.
- Pasta.
- Potato.
- Tuna (or flaked fish in general).
- Minced meat dishes (e.g. chilli).
- Home-made breads.
- Pizza and bases.
- Cakes.
- Home-made biscuits.

The list is endless, and with some imagination you will be able to come up with some sensational but bizarre ideas.

In addition, you could try coloured light bulbs and drapes.

FOLLOW-UP

As this could be a most interesting evening, you should follow it up with either a more bizarre evening or a more sedate one. Whatever you do, you will have a group of people willing to attend something else, and your follow-up could be on those lines.

16 'Come Dancing' Evening

Ballroom dancing, though popular for many years, peaked in its popularity through the 70s with the *Come Dancing* series on TV. Since then it has somewhat declined in popularity, though it is still a preferred activity of older people. This is an ideal way to reach out to the older generation. They will fondly remember the dances they went to and try to recreate the dream!

PLANNING

First, book a good-sized hall and an excellent leader. The hall is very important because if it is too small, the floor will become very congested. The leader is also very important as he or she (or preferably both) will need to help your guests go through the steps. Also, if you choose the right leaders, they will help people by dancing with them, and will, if asked nicely, give a demonstration of classical ballroom dancing as part of the fee.

Finding the right leaders, however, could present a problem. Ask around and be prepared to search for someone who is well-liked and respected. Your local library will be a good place to start. Unless you really want the event to end up as an over-70s do, try to get a younger couple to lead for you, thus emphasizing on your invitations that the dance is for people of all ages.

When considering your invitations, do think about what particular age group you are aiming at. This will determine the sort of price (if any!) you want to charge your guests, and what sort of food and drink you will make available. Of course, there are many young people who enjoy ballroom dancing, and you might want to make the event specifically for under-50s. If you are brave – and your youth group is up for it – you could make it for under-25s (you may be shocked by how many young people want to try their hand at this sort of dancing!).

Finally, make sure you have an adequate PA system that will provide sound for CDs and LPs (remember them?). The music is likely to be pre-recorded (can you afford a live big band sound?) and your leaders will have a fair idea of the system they will require.

GUESTS

Guests will primarily be those who are interested in ballroom dancing. Try to have as many couples as possible so that everyone has a partner. Don't limit yourselves to one age group unless that is the specific aim of your outreach at that time. Get as broad a range of ages as possible so that young people can mix with older people. This cross-generational evening could be very beneficial for the community, as well as the church. In fact, your youth group could host this evening for you. If this is the case, they will want to demonstrate some of their own dancing skills to an older generation. Many youngsters learn tap dancing and jazz dancing – skills that many in the older generation still admire.

COST

The cost of the hall and the leaders will be the most expensive part of this evening. Of course, if you have food and drink there will be additional costs involved, but you could offset these costs by charging for the event or, alternatively, just for the food and drink people buy on the night.

VARIATIONS

Why not vary the theme by introducing different eras?

- A 40s 'Glen Miller' evening, with appropriate wartime food.

- A 50s jive night.

- A 60s 'do the twist' night.

- A 70s disco night.

17 Cookery Demonstration

Before we get into the detail of this event, I would like to defend its inclusion in the book. I have been spurred on by the incredible success of Delia Smith's basic cookery book, as seen on TV. Despite being pilloried by her peers for the basic nature of the book (how to boil an egg, etc.), it appears that sales have proved her assessment that many people in society cannot do the basic things. Pre-prepared meals are a multi-million pound industry, and the popularity of fast food is growing by the day. This speaks to two problem areas: our laziness and our inability to cook for ourselves. Many people are leaving home never having been taught how to cook simple meals, and some schools no longer teach cooking to their pupils. The success of Delia's book shows a desire for basic knowledge. The opportunity is to help people who wish to be helped, as well as build relationships with them.

PLANNING

First ask yourself who this demonstration is aimed at. The answer to that question will determine your planning route. For example, if you decide this is a demonstration for housewives, you could plan a morning session when the children have gone to school. There are many different sectors to aim at: single men, students, young mothers, old people, young married couples, and so on.

Having decided which group you are aiming at, you will

then be able to decide the sort of foods you need to prepare. For example, choosing students means that offering an evening that shows them how to cook meals for six for under £6 might be useful. Well-planned recipes will help everyone take full advantage of the session.

Then there is the question of venue. If you are planning a morning for mothers, you will be able to keep the setting informal and cosy. With students, you might want to use a more basic kitchen, since most student kitchens are pretty basic. The choice of venue will also determine how many people you can invite. If you are in the cosy setting, then you can really only invite up to six people, otherwise no one will be able to see.

Let me summarize:

1. Decide who to aim at.

2. Decide what to prepare.

3. Decide where you will hold the event.

So, having decided these three points, we now come to what we will do during the event itself. For the sake of ease, I intend to follow the student line as an example.

The proposition is to prepare meals for six for under £6. Plan about three menus that offer variety, and allow your guests the opportunity to explore for themselves. This will cause you to be creative and thoughtful. Think carefully about the equipment you will use. It is no good talking about equipment that students will never have access to or cannot afford. On the other hand, it would be good to include a discussion on the sorts of basic equipment worth investing in. The types of food you will need to be looking at in terms of recipe are pizza and pasta, pastry and pies, rice, Eastern food and the humble potato.

Try to be enterprising. There are some ways in which you

can benefit from the retailers' desire to attract customers. For example, you may find that one of the supermarkets will 'sponsor' your event by donating food if you push their name. They may give you vouchers or samples for your guests to try. Nothing ventured, nothing gained!

Finally, try to ensure that this event is as hands-on as possible. Each guest should be able to try to do something. In addition, each guest should have time to sample the wonderful food you have all prepared. But remember to allow ample time for washing-up afterwards!

GUESTS

The guests you invite will be determined by your answers to the first few questions above. Having decided who, what and where, you will have a much more defined target group of people, which you should stick to as carefully as possible. For example, if you choose housewives for a morning session, it may be inappropriate for your male curate to attend just because he likes the idea of sampling the food!

COST

The cost of the event will obviously depend on the menus you are preparing. So if you have planned a student six for £6 evening, three meals will only cost you £18 (you cannot cheat!). Other costs might include refreshments and possibly a book related to the topic.

VARIATIONS

In the summer you could hold a barbecue demonstration for men. (How many burnt offerings have you been to?) Vegetarianism is increasingly popular, and some ideas in this area are always welcome. You could look at children's party food or Christmas menus, etc. The variations are endless. Be as creative as you want and have a great time!

18 Craft Show

In any church there will be people who can carve, knit and paint – to mention just a few basic crafts. So the idea here is to organize and promote a craft show, exhibiting crafts made by members of your congregation.

PLANNING

The first thing is to identify what is readily available to you. Very often you will be surprised at the skills your people have. Do not assume that simply because you do not know about their hobbies and interests they do not have any. Having identified what is available, decide if you have enough to organize a show. If you don't, there are some interesting alternatives to consider.

The first alternative is to pool your talents with other team churches if you are in a team church or parish. Alternatively, you will find that those with craft skills in your church will probably have friends and contacts who are also crafts people. In the spirit of reaching out, why not invite them to be involved with the show? After all, if nothing else happens, you will begin to develop relationships with these people and their families. A further spin-off will be that people in your church will be affirmed in their hobbies and will enjoy introducing their other friends to their church friends.

Once you have found the talent in your church, you will be in a position to set a date and start planning the day. First on the list is the decision about where the event will take place, and the availability of the venue will, to some extent, determine the date of the event. If you have a church hall, this will be easier than hiring a hall, but if you need to hire a venue try the local community centre, library or school.

As a first-time effort, you might want to limit your event to two or three hours so that you can see how well it works. Give yourself a few weeks to plan. You will find that an event like this could get local paper coverage, so market it to the community. Talk to your local tourist office as they may well promote it or know how to get into your local council newsletters. If you have good connections, you could ask your local councillor or celebrity to open the show. Again, this will give you maximum publicity. Giving yourself time will allow you the space to explore these opportunities.

Look into leaflet and poster publicity. Very often you can place leaflets in public places like libraries. Depending on the crafts to be exhibited, you could target parts of the community. Hosting the show in a local school will offer different possibilities to hosting it in an old age care home. In any event, make sure that you and your friends publicize the show as much as possible.

As part of the event, you should include that most wonderful of crafts: cake- and biscuit-making. This will give you the opportunity to have tea and coffee with the results of that craft! It also means that rather than people simply walking round and then out, you can sit and chat with those who come to look. As this is an outreach event, you will find that this will offer you the opportunity to follow up contacts.

Decide what, if anything, is to be for sale. This could help fund the day, but could be difficult to administer. Be sure that you have a clear policy on this, because if you do not, then someone else will make the decision for you.

GUESTS

Obviously the people exhibiting will want to bring family and friends. This will account for some of the people attending, but many will have to be reached through publicity. There are many other calls on people's time, so make sure that your show is well marketed – and worth coming to!

COST

Cost will depend on the hire of the hall and how much you spend on publicity. The only other cost should be that of drinks and (unless you do include it as a craft) food. You may decide to charge for entrance, but this will limit the venues you can use, and will demand that your show be of a high enough standard to make the fee worth paying. Alternatively, you could charge an entrance fee and donate it to a local charity.

VARIATIONS

You could offer an auction at the end of the event, with proceeds going to the charity of your choice. I would suggest that you do not use it for your church building fund, as this is primarily about outreach – not church funding. It will show that you are interested in the local community.

OUR EXPERIENCE

We have so far held one such show. We were surprised by the talent in our church that we had never found before. We were also surprised by the interest shown. We held the show in our own hall on a Saturday morning for three hours. We offered food and drink, and had about forty people come. For a first effort we were pleased with the result – especially as this brought in quite a few people we had never met before.

19 Day Trips

PLANNING

An organized day trip to an event, place or attraction will require meticulous and organized planning well in advance. First, the venue has to be agreed. A day trip to the seaside or to an attraction like Alton Towers, or perhaps a trip into the countryside can have lots of opportunities and will be enjoyed by many people.

Having agreed the venue, you should do three things immediately:

1. Check with your church leadership that your day trip will not clash with anything they are planning.

2. Call the venue or the local tourist office to ensure that it will be open and that there are no other problems anticipated for the date you wish to go.

3. Call a recognized and approved bus company to book a bus for the day.

Once you have done this you will know the cost of the trip (that is, the cost of entry – if there is one – and the cost of the coach). You can then calculate the cost of the trip for adults and children. Only when this has been done are you ready to announce your trip. If you don't work out your costs carefully there will always be someone wanting to negotiate a better price. My advice is: don't do it! On another financial point, always take the money with the booking. All too often you will end up chasing money, and this is often a cause of embarrassment for both parties.

Consider your marketing strategy! Church bulletin boards, parish magazines and news sheets are all very helpful tools, so use them. In addition, you may have to visit other cell groups to talk to people if you need to include other cell groups. Remember that while many people receive their news sheets not many read them, and those who do read them may not take the information on board. In addition, most Christians seem to operate on a 'just in time' basis. This can cause two problems:

1. *You* panic when you still haven't sold more than half your seats a week beforehand.

2. *They* panic when you tell them that you are booked up and cannot take anyone else.

Of course, your church is not like this, so you will not come up against this. However, just in case it does happen, be prepared to push, wheedle, bully, plead and generally make a nuisance of yourself!

GUESTS

You should start with your own cell group and include them in the day. Then you can begin to open it up to other groups and members of your church. The people who will be interested will be determined by the event you are organizing. For instance, our church is organizing a coach trip to Chessington, followed by a concert. This will be of interest not only to teenagers and 20-somethings, but also to people of my age with slightly younger aged children (I am now in my late 30s and need my children to justify the trip and cost, even though secretly I want to go!).

COST

The cost will be determined by the following factors:

- Entry fee (if any).
- Coach hire.
- Marketing (if any).

If you are going to an attraction, you will find that there are group reductions and often cheaper entry for the organizers (this is worked out on the basis of the food and drink consumed by your group in the attraction itself). Other than these costs, those who go will have to decide whether to take sandwiches and drinks or buy on site.

VARIATIONS

There are so many variations to this event, and you will know your locality and the surroundings better than anyone else will.

OUR EXPERIENCE

This event should really be a church-wide event, because unless you are going in a minibus there will be plenty of room on the coach. It is a great means of building relationships as there is time to chat on the coach and while you are wandering around the attraction. We have taken coach trips to London to see a show and trips to France with smaller groups. We have had success with large and small groups.

20 Five-a-Side Football

In order to have any credibility in planning and hosting this event, you will need to be able to field a decent team of your own from church. Also, I would suggest that you have a reason for hosting the event – maybe a good charity to which the monies could be donated.

PLANNING

Give yourself about six weeks to plan this event. Booking the venue is the most important thing. Most venues prefer not to book more than one week in advance, but if you explain what you are trying to achieve, the manager and staff should be quite helpful. Indeed, they may well help advertise the event with the teams that normally use their facilities.

In reality, for one full evening or afternoon's competition, you will need about eight teams. Allow ten minutes per game (five minutes each way), and make it a knockout competition. This will mean that you finish in about one and a half hours. Sixteen teams in a knockout competition will double the time it takes. If you have between eight and sixteen teams, you will need to look at creative ways to get to a knockout stage as quickly but fairly as possible.

As you will not know many of the teams, organize a draw to sort out the competition and the matches. Do not forget to nominate a referee – the place you hire may be helpful in this regard, unless you already know someone who would make a good referee. You will also need to have an appropriate prize for the eventual winners (something that all five team members can enjoy).

So, having thought out all the details of the event itself, decide how you are going to get enough teams to participate. This will mean choosing with care the charity you will support. It will also mean inviting (either in person or by letter) the sorts of people you are trying to reach.

One way of doing this is to write to organizations inviting them to your church's five-a-side football challenge in support of . . . . If you invite people this way, you will need to follow it up, or use contacts you already have. Organizations such as schools, larger businesses or retailers are ideal to invite as they will have a larger pool of people to draw on.

A second way to invite people along is to organize eight men (or women) to arrange their own teams and play each other in competition. This way, each group member who wants to participate gets to invite his or her own friends to the championship. This will help build their own friendships and give them opportunity to invite their friends to other exciting events.

A third way may well be to issue challenges to other organizations without the problems of running a championship. This will mean that fewer people are involved, but if you could get 20 players, you could rotate the teams through the event. This gives opportunity for people to talk and get to know each other. Again, schools or places of work are great starting points.

Finally, why not try to create a five-a-side team to compete in the local leagues? If getting to know people is important, then take the time to play sport in their own leagues. You can gain much respect and people will try to get to know you. The biggest problem with this route is that despite good intentions it is very tempting to end up working on already existing relationships within your team.

GUESTS

As this is a great game for people of most ages and either sex, you should try to get a good mix of players from about 16 through to about 45 to 50, both male and female.

COST

The cost of a competition should be no more than £3 per person, depending on the cost of venue hire and the prize you buy. Supposing a £3 limit, most players will pay their own cost, especially if some of it goes to a charity, say £1 per player. This means that the cost to the church is minimal. Some individuals may wish to pay for their whole team.

VARIATIONS

If you are a big enough church, you could try to place a team in the local Saturday morning leagues. You could even combine with other churches to do this.

Other than five-a-side soccer, you could try volleyball (great fun and good for mixed teams), indoor cricket or indoor hockey (violent when played with mixed teams, but fun nonetheless).

OUR EXPERIENCE

In the past we have been involved in eleven-a-side inter-church leagues and we are now involved in a mixed church team in the local leagues. We have not been able to go any further than simply 'having a presence', though we have hosted dinners for all players where the gospel has been clearly preached.

We have also played five-a-side with other non-Christian teams and have had a thoroughly good time, being able to reach out, especially afterwards. It is the hour or so after the game that is so important (as is the fact that you as a team have been fair and clean during the game!). It is during that hour that many good friendships have been made – friendships that are still being built on.

21 Food/Drink Stall in Your Town

This 'event' has many advantages to it – and many pitfalls. First, it allows you to reach vast numbers of people in your town centre, but it does not allow you to grow friendships at the time of meeting. Secondly, it is not that difficult to achieve, but you do need to plan carefully. Thirdly, it allows your church to be visible to the community, but you will need your community's permission to proceed. Finally, everyone in your church can get involved (an advantage and disadvantage rolled into one!).

PLANNING

In planning, think about when is the best time to be on the streets offering free food and drink. If you are in a seaside town, you might be interested in the summer months when there are many people around. You might want to give out cold drinks in the summer, or hot soup in the winter. You may want to offer small snacks (popcorn, biscuits, etc.) or nibbles for people to eat. The time of year you choose will, to some extent, determine what you offer. For the purpose of this chapter, I am going to concentrate on the opportunities in the winter.

First, have a good look round your town centre and choose your site carefully. You will need a site that is busy, but not in the way of local shoppers or traders, and you should be a fair way from any food outlets (they will not be best pleased if you open your stall by their door!). Easy access for deliveries through the day is important, as is an electrical supply if possible.

Having chosen your site, approach your local council for permission. Take a full plan with you and explain what you are trying to do. You will need their permission before you go ahead, but before they give it they will need to know that you are not intending to be a nuisance. You should also inform your local police so that they do not try to move you on. As in all these sorts of events, it is better to check before-hand than to annoy the local authorities and have to pack everything away.

Assuming that everyone is happy and the date has been agreed, get your stall together. Trestle tables with covers will be the easiest 'counter tops' to move around, and you could either use a V-shape next to a wall (two tables) or a triangle or square shape. This will partly depend on the space you have available.

Next, decide what you are going to offer. If it is winter and the date is close to Christmas, I would suggest warm soup and bread. You will need some way of heating your soup (perhaps several Calor Gas stoves and pans) and somewhere to store your food safely (away from birds, etc.). If you can keep a car or van nearby, this will be the answer. Make sure you have a constant supply of soup and bread. You may even want to have several sorts of soup. Powder soups will be easiest, but then you need a good close water supply. You will be constantly boiling and keeping warm pans of soup, hence the need for more than one cooker. You will find that the soup disappears very quickly, so keep it on the heat all the time.

Make sure you have plenty of plastic or cardboard cups with holders (if needed), lots of kitchen roll, and a waste bin nearby (you do not want to damage your reputation by having lots of rubbish on the streets from your stand). Arrange for some music in the background to attract attention, and some posters announcing free soup and bread. You could use your church banner as a 'sign'.

Finally, recruit lots of helpers. In addition to those serving, people will be needed to fetch and carry, and to keep cleaning up the area around you.

On the spiritual level, have a group of people prepared to stand and talk to those who come for their free soup and bread. It is important that you have another event shortly after the day, possibly a concert or personality speaker, in order for you to be able to invite people into your church as close to the day as possible. If it is winter and close to Christmas, you might be inviting them to your special Christmas concert with your big name guest speaker.

You should also have church leaflets available, telling people about yourselves, what you do and when you do it. Each member of the team needs to be prepared to pray for people, or talk at length about Jesus. This really is a full gospel opportunity that needs to be taken. You should certainly have literature like *Why Jesus?* or *Journey into Life* available and Alpha course details.

COST

Your local wholesaler will be the best place to go for cheaper prices on food, drink, cups, etc. By focusing on particular food and drinks, you can buy in bulk, which is cheaper.

VARIATIONS

The variations you can achieve are based on the time of year you decide to hold this event. In the summer, you could tie in some street acts (juggling, clowns, music) as part of the fun, or you could add in more direct gospel activities such as drama and sketchboards. In the winter, you could tie in a gift-wrapping stand (see Event 13). At Easter, you could offer hot cross buns. What about relating your food and drink to a particular sporting theme? The choice is as endless as your imagination!

22 Freshers Week

Many students go to university for the first time with a mix of excitement, anticipation and fear. For many this will be the first time away from home, and during the first weeks they feel vulnerable. If you can arrange a welcome team that helps carry luggage and provides refreshments, you will be a most welcome group. Further, there is opportunity during the Freshers week to work with the Christian Union groups in the university. Friendship and help are the two most attractive things you can offer during the first weeks.

PLANNING

The timing for this 'event' will obviously be during the first few weeks of the academic year. To find out when that is, call your local college bursar, who will also be able to tell you what activities are planned. If you have a good contact with the Christian Union, you should plan well ahead with them to arrange the details of what you could do to help.

Here are some suggestions:

1. Luggage carriers. Many students will arrive and need the very practical help of simply carrying baggage from the car. Arrange a team of helpers to be on hand. You should only help those who agree to your help! During the course of the day, you will get many opportunities to talk

to and befriend people. Keep a supply of simple cards with you (see below) to give away to remind people about you and your church.

2. Tea/coffee-makers. Most halls of residence have facilities for tea- and coffee-making. If not, take your own equipment. Simply provide cups of tea and coffee (at your expense) and any home-made cakes that you can get your group to make. A friendly smile and a cup of tea can help put both parents' and students' minds at ease.

3. Meals. You should ask a number of people within the church to be prepared to host a welcome meal on at least one evening, and certainly on the first few Sundays. These people need not be families. If you have an active 20-something group, you could organize them into small groups to arrange meals. Every student you come across during the first few weeks should be invited to a meal somewhere in your church. It is a habit that should be encouraged, so that all new faces in the congregation can be offered a meal.

4. Welcome team. Try going around the halls of residence with a welcome pack for your town. Ask the students if they are settling down and whether they need any help. You can offer them the pack with places of interest, the cheapest places to eat and drink, and a little about the shopping in town. Of course, the pack should also contain information about your church.

5. Organized activities. This is a great time to try other ideas in this book. Paintballing, Laser Quest, ten-pin bowling and barbecues are all great activities to put on and invite students to. If you can create good relationships in the first few weeks, you can keep in touch with them for much longer.

6.   Freshers week. Most universities have a Student Union-
     run 'market-place' where different groups can advertise
     their activities. Working with the Christian Union, you
     could advertise the activities you are hosting through the
     market-place.

I have mentioned giving out a welcome card or pack from
your church. This should outline your regular activities,
especially those for students. You should include at least one
or two major events taking place during the first two to three
weeks (maybe some of the ideas suggested in point 5 above).
Finally, there should be a helpline number – perhaps the
church telephone number. Many students do get very lonely
and homesick in the first weeks of term.
     For more ideas of what to do and how to help, you may
want to contact UCCF (38 De Montfort Street, Leicester,
LE1 7GP). There are also some excellent books on the
subject of leaving home for the first time and becoming a
student.
     Remember that the principle of this outreach idea is not
to preach the gospel as a four-point salvation message, but
rather to befriend and help. You will find that once a level of
trust is built, you will be able to talk to people about the
gospel. They will listen to you more once you have proved
your trust and friendship.
     In planning, you will need to be aware of the cost in terms
of people. Such an event is very labour intensive, and you
need your best people, not just those who are available.

COST

This will depend on how far you choose to go. If you stick
at simply providing tea, coffee and cakes, the only real cost
will be the printing of cards. The more activities you offer,
the higher the cost will be. When planning your events,

remember that most students will be concerned about cost, so do not organize expensive activities unless you are willing to sponsor them.

VARIATIONS

Talk to the students already in your church. Ask them what they needed in their first weeks and respond to those needs.

OUR EXPERIENCE

We have had good relationships at the local college for some time and have seen a number of students join us during their time at college. We are just beginning to look at how to reach out to the first-year students on a long-term basis, but the ideas above come from my own personal experience of college life or from other churches that have active outreach to the Freshers.

23 Games Night

PLANNING

Once an evening has been chosen, the next thing to choose is what you will be playing. You can go one of several routes:

1. Long board games, e.g. Monopoly. In choosing this sort of evening, you will need to be clear that as these games can take up to three hours to play, you will be effectively segregating your guests for the evening.

2. Short board games, e.g. Othello. This means that you will be able to have short games and mix up the players after every game. If your intention is to get everyone to meet everyone else, then this will work for you. You could even introduce a 'league' and offer prizes.

3. Card games. Here you can either be game specific (e.g. bridge) or allow your guests to play different games. This is also a great way of learning new games, and letting your guests take an active part as they teach you new games.

4. Party games (e.g. charades or party board games). Most people now own at least one fun party game and most people are willing to play them (at least once anyway!). This is a good way of breaking down barriers. We have found that men versus women teams have created some excellent games with tension and fun. It definitely brings out the competitive edge!

Whichever option you choose, be sure to plan the games in advance. Too many evenings of this nature have floundered because no one checked beforehand that the games were immediately to hand – and that someone knew how to play them!

Decide whether you are going to provide food and drinks. This event is so much more enjoyable if you offer pizzas and other food rather than just nibbles. If you decide to go for a theme night, there are some excellent German games now available, and a German night with food to match could be great fun.

GUESTS

Your cell group can decide for themselves who to invite – an evening in someone's home could include up to 20 people if you have enough rooms. The excellent thing about the card evening in particular is that it is not age specific. In fact the wider the age difference the better, as many older people have an excellent store of good absorbing games.

COST

Cost should be as close to zero as possible. If you bring in nibbles, keep it simple and cheap. After all, your guests are coming to play games, not score you on your food. If you are going to have more substantial offerings, these could be home made and cheap – home-made pizzas should cost no more than £3 to make. Ask members of your group to bring food so that the cost is spread.

VARIATIONS

In addition to the options already mentioned, what about having a children's party for adults (e.g. pinning the tail on the donkey)?

OUR EXPERIENCE

We have found games nights to vary in terms of success. If the mix of guests is such that there are a few people there who do not wish to participate, the evening can be hard to keep going. If there are several people there who go over the top, it can be hard to keep the evening on track. Therefore, a good mix of people has helped us.

24 Gardening Demonstration

PLANNING

Because this event will be unusual for most churches, it will need to be well planned. Further, it should be a hands-on demonstration that all can participate in.

First, a date needs to be set which is convenient for all concerned. You might need to book a local professional gardener if you do not have someone in your church capable of running such an event. Or you might want to book a local garden centre for the event, where all the facilities are on site for you. Consider preparing some literature for guests to take away for future reference. These events lend themselves to low-key evangelism or literature handouts, so think about the level of presentation you are going to give. As this event is going to be of interest to a lot of people, consider putting an advert in your local newspaper. At the very least you will make some new contacts.

GUESTS

Young or old, most people will have some interest in their garden. The specific type of gardening event you put on (see below) will determine the sort of people you should invite, and whether it will be a large event in a garden centre or a small event in your front room.

COST

Cost will depend on three things:

- Food and drink: if you wish to put on food and drink then some cost will be incurred.

- Materials: you will need to buy some materials to demonstrate with and for your guests to have a go.

- Location: if you can tie this evening in with a local garden centre or professional gardener, you might find that provided they can sell stock the centre/gardener will 'sponsor' either the whole or part of the event for you, thus reducing your costs.

VARIATIONS

- Hanging baskets.
- Potted plants.
- Window boxes (excellent for elderly people or those living in flats).
- Water gardening.
- Garden planning.
- Questions and answers (à la *Gardeners' Question Time* on BBC Radio 4).
- Fruit and/or vegetable gardening.

FOLLOW-UP

This is an ideal evening in which to hand out leaflets to guests – the church leaflet, an Alpha course leaflet or a concert/event leaflet. This allows guests to read at their own leisure. It is also ideal for a small five-minute gospel talk on some aspect of God's creative work (without the cringe factor, please!).

25 Golf Tournament and Breakfast

PLANNING

In the first instance, determine how many people would be interested in a golf tournament. In most churches there will be a number of golfers, male and female, and I suspect that you could well be oversubscribed if you are not careful!

Next, arrange a date (preferably at the weekend when most people are free) and book the course. I would suggest a nine-hole tournament, as this keeps the time down to a minimum. You could either book an 18-hole course, making it clear that you are interested in only playing nine holes, or you could go to a more specialized nine-hole course that will be ideal for you. Book as many tee times as you need (if you are playing in fours and anticipate 20 people in total, you will need five tee times). Obviously, if you are a club member, or if a friend or someone from your cell group is, booking will be easier, and possibly cheaper!

Then you need to book a breakfast for the people who are playing. Your tee time will decide what time breakfast should be. If you have an early start, have breakfast after your game. If you have a late tee time, then you could have breakfast first. It may be possible to have a private room at the course clubhouse. If so, this would be ideal. If not, you may have to book into a local hotel or restaurant. This does complicate matters, as you will have to be more precise in your timing.

I would be inclined to take a straw poll of who might be

interested and will bring a friend along, and then book tee times and breakfast accordingly. You can always cancel a tee time or a couple of breakfasts if necessary. It is harder to add people in at a later stage.

Having planned all this, decide on the rules of the game. You could choose to play as individuals, with the best score winning, or in twos. It really is up to you, provided you are within the course rules. I would strongly advise you to have thought about this before you get to the tees and to have the right number of prizes for the winners. Because you are only playing nine holes, and there may be a few of you, the possibility of drawing is very high. You need to anticipate this with a tiebreak or a few extra prizes.

At the breakfast, make sure there are no 'in groups' of friends. This is disastrous for friendship-building and will undo all your hard work on the course. You could have a short talk about sport and the gospel, or about your Alpha course, but if you do, try not to make it intense and heavy.

Finally, if you wanted to and could afford it, you could book the course pro to go round the course with you to teach and advise (unless he happens to be a friend or member of your church, in which case you might like to ask him to organize the event for you!).

GUESTS

As mentioned above, this is a great mixed-sex sport, and you could have mixed teams. It would be good to have guests of both sexes, as this makes the game much more interesting. You will also find that there is a huge age span, and you should really encourage this. You will find that golfers now come in all sorts of shapes, ages and sizes, as many young people are turning to the game. Think about giving golf handicaps to your guests, thus ensuring interest for everyone.

COST

The cost will depend on the course you choose to play on, and where you have breakfast. Local golfers will be able to tell you where to play the cheapest rounds of golf if cost is a problem. If you explain to the course administrator that many of your guests have never played on the course before, they may be interested in reducing their fees in order to gain new long-term custom.

VARIATIONS

There are some great variations on this theme. First, you could arrange a golf master class for the morning. This may limit the number of people you can invite, but it will be interesting for all. Focused time well spent will help your friends improve their swing or putting (you could focus on one of those areas if you wished). Alternatively, you could host a driving competition on a driving range. This is a much cheaper option, and may allow you to invite more people.

If you wish to go really down market, you could of course host a pitch and putt or a crazy golf competition. While this is not for the purists, it is good fun and creates many laughs. Finally, for the really incompetent golfers, why not host a carpet golf competition in your home?

26 Ground Force Day

Sometimes outreach can take the form of helping people in areas where they have difficulty. Gardening is an excellent example of this. By getting a few people together from your cell group, you can have a lot of fun clearing, digging and planting while helping people. And there are plenty of people who do need help: the elderly, the sick, the disabled and single parents.

PLANNING

In terms of planning, it would be so helpful if you could choose a nice warm day, but unfortunately there's no way of guaranteeing this. What you can guarantee is a team spirit and heaps of fun. Make sure you agree a day that is convenient to all concerned so that everyone will turn up on the day. It is a good idea to have a team leader with some basic gardening know-how, such as pruning skills!

Ensure you have enough tools for everyone, and something in which to take rubbish away. As a further thought, you may need to check when your local tip is open so that you don't waste valuable time.

Finally, you do need to ensure that you have adequate food and drink available, though the person whose garden you are working on may want to provide this. If they do, encourage them because it helps to build relationship and partnership, which can be very important.

GUESTS

I suppose that 'guest' is the wrong word here – 'volunteer' is better! Having worked out who you are going to help, sort out your volunteers. You may have to 'persuade' some people, but that can be great fun too. (Use the guilt trip – it works every time!) If you can, use families or a wide range of people. This helps your host to realize that the church is made up of many different kinds of people. You might find that some sensitivity is needed – elderly people can be concerned about having young people in their gardens.

COST

The total cost of this event should be zero, unless you want to pay for new plants, food and drink.

VARIATIONS

You can use the same ideas for:

• Decorating – inside and out.

• Building work.

• Shopping for people.

OUR EXPERIENCE

We have often helped people within cell groups to decorate, and have worked on gardens. Volunteers can be hard to come by, and in some instances their work has been less than helpful. Wisdom is needed. Having said that, we have been successful in breaking down barriers and building new friendships.

27 Internet Night

This event aims to teach people about the Internet and looks at sites of particular interest.

PLANNING

Having chosen the evening for your event, pick the venue carefully. There are two considerations here. First, do you wish the evening to be for a small number of people (say around six to seven people) or do you intend it to be for a large group of people (say twelve to fourteen)? The former will allow much more hands-on participation, so it is probably more attractive. It will take less planning too.

Working on the basis that the smaller event is better, the second consideration to take into account when fixing a venue is accessibility to the computer(s). Someone's home will work well if there is enough room for the people you invite. Ideally there would be two telephone lines so that you could set up a couple of computers (one could be a lap top).

Having access to the necessary hardware, you then need someone to guide you through the labyrinth of sites now available. There's bound to be an expert within your own ranks or you could approach someone from a computer store. Spend time discussing with the guide the sorts of things you want to look at during the event. These could include talking about the equipment needed, and the better

109

hardware and software. You could talk about the possibility of putting barriers into the system to prevent children looking at unsuitable sites. Other ideas might be how to use a chat room, or deal with chat room problems. In particular, you could talk about the various providers and the advantages they offer. Finally, you could talk about how the Internet works and how to find your way around it.

You will also need to look at some interesting sites. These could be interest sites (soccer/news, etc.), shopping sites, sites to help your children research their homework — the list is endless. Looking at the best of the children's sites can help parents to feel more comfortable about their children and the Internet. Other things you could look at might be how to download from the Net, how to buy on the Net, and how to get the best from it. If the people you invite are interested, you could look at making your own website. Indeed, this could be the subject of one whole evening.

GUESTS

Many people are very interested in the Internet and how to use it. Some are parents whose children are so advanced in Net technology that they feel left behind. Many people are bewildered and make elementary mistakes on the Net, often giving it up as too confusing. There are also many people who are worried by the Net and don't know where to start. All these people will make ideal guests for the evening. It would be unhelpful to have too many experts present at the event as the language could soon become very technical and out of everyone else's depth.

You might want to make this a family affair. There is no reason why you should not invite children as well as adults. Children have no fear of the Net, and explore for fun, so the evening could be made very interesting by their presence.

COST

Cost will be very low, apart from refreshments. In addition you might want to offer some of the relevant magazines available for people to look at, though your guide will provide most of the software you will need. The only real cost is the telephone call for the connection, but to be honest it is unlikely to bankrupt anyone!

VARIATIONS

As mentioned above you could always spend one evening building your own website. This would be very helpful and educational, as well as fun! You could also look at a games night where a different sort of guide could review the various games available. This is particularly helpful in the pre-Christmas season when parents are struggling to find appropriate games for their children. You could extend this idea to look at the hardware available, especially for first-time buyers, or to help parents upgrade joysticks and accessories.

Finally, you could have an evening looking for particular theme sites (football/live events, etc.) or finance on the Web. There are so many variations, and these grow daily as new ideas spring up on the Net!

OUR EXPERIENCE

As a family we have found it necessary to look carefully at the Net, partly because of curious and nosey children. We have found that talking to other parents about sites and opportunities (as well as problems) has helped us and encouraged us. The opportunities are endless, but the concerns are great. We have also spent time with others helping them around the Net, though we ourselves have only a basic understanding of it. My own view is that many people want to learn, but do not want to commit to a six-week evening class, so why not offer them a one-off lesson to help them and whet their appetite?

28 It's a Knockout!

This is a fun event, whereby teams compete against one another in simple sports, obstacle races or other challenges. Ideally, you can use this event to include entire families and many friends, or an inter-cell group competition will offer lots of opportunities to get to know each other. It is noticeable that once people have laughed together, they seem to have a better all round relationship.

PLANNING

This will require lots of planning, and your group will be kept busy for some time. If you are planning a family event, a Saturday or Sunday afternoon will be the most convenient time.

Decide how many games to play, and what is required to play them. You will need teams (hence the inter-cell group idea works better), and thus will need several sets of props. For example, if you have six teams, you will need six sets of everything. Bear in mind that it is better to have too many games rather than not enough. You might want to use the same games for adults and children – two sets of games with points added together for the end result. (See below for game ideas.)

A score board is required and someone to update it, and one central person who can keep the event moving and everyone involved. You could also assign one person to take the incriminating photos!

Finally, pray for great weather – or make sure that you can move the games inside if necessary.

GUESTS

Families will really enjoy this event, especially those with younger children (between five and eleven). Outside of this, you can invite anyone you like. Be clear as to the nature of the event. Some people don't enjoy this sort of thing, so a clear invite will avoid embarrassment.

Make the event as big as you can manage. Three to four cell groups with ten people each plus guests will make around 60 people including children, and a great atmosphere that everyone will enjoy should result.

COST

Most of the games can be sorted out at low cost using home-based materials that are easy to find or cheap to buy. You can also use many natural obstacles that will increase the fun and difficulty. Food can take the form of a picnic, so no cost there, unless you fancy offering a pre-planned barbecue for the price of a ticket (thus recouping your costs).

VARIATIONS

There are many fun games you can use:

- Dribbling footballs around a crazy obstacle course.

- Carrying buckets of water across obstacles and measuring what's left.

- Blindfolded custard tart throwing or wet sponge throwing.

- Carrying armfuls of bean bags across obstacles, etc.

- Building a small platform that has to be stood on out of basic materials scattered around the area.

- Traditional school sports day events: sack race; egg and spoon race; wheelbarrow race.

Basically, use anything you can think of. Rerun some of the wacky events they use in the Channel 5 revival of this 70s TV programme and adapt them to your style – the more outlandish the better! Do not worry about making people look like absolute idiots. The more fun you make of each other, the more everyone will enjoy themselves.

29 Jazz Night

PLANNING

First decide which band to book. I would suggest a good three- or four-piece band is more than sufficient for most events. If you do not know where to start to look for a good jazz band, you need to call the main Christian record companies (Kingsway, Word, Alliance, ICC, etc.) or the main Christian music magazines (*Cross Rhythms*, etc.). The record companies will be interested in promoting their own artists, whereas the magazines will be more objective and may have a wider contact base. In all events, the band you book should be recommended and should be willing to talk about their faith.

When you book the band, be sure to talk to them about:

- PA: Who is providing it? It is better if they provide the PA and engineer because this way they get exactly what they need. You also need to agree a price for the PA (it will not come free!) and the engineer.

- Lighting: Will they need any special lighting? They probably won't, but it is better to be sure.

- On-the-day arrangements: When will they arrive? What and when will they need to eat? What will they need while playing (water, etc.)?

- Advertising: Do they have posters you could use? What is the full name of the band? Do they have a biography or press pack you could use? Could you have an album to play on local radio?

- Payment: What are you paying for and when will they expect payment? (Usually on the night, after the event.)

- Album sales: Who has the rights to sell any albums and merchandise?

The other main decision to make is where to hold the event. As this is a jazz night, informality is the name of the game. I would suggest that you hire a large room where you can seat guests around tables in groups of six to eight. Your church hall may be big enough, or you may need to hire a local hall. Wherever you book, you must be able to 'decorate' it a little (use of lighting is very important and atmosphere can be created with drapes, etc.). You may want to go to the extreme of booking a function room in a hotel or pub. These tend to be dark and have tables and the right atmosphere for a good jazz night. On a practical level, you will need access to the venue about four hours before the event.

Make sure that the venue is licensed for such events and that they have adequate insurance. You may need a special licence, or you may need to have extra insurance. It is your responsibility as the organizer to make sure that all the legal requirements are covered. Your local council offices will be able to help you in this area.

Your choice of band and venue will determine the success of the event. If you have a great band but a venue with no atmosphere, there will be a very flat response to the event. The same is true the other way round.

Once you have worked out all your costs, you will be able to set a ticket price that is as low as possible while covering your expenses.

Having booked your band and the venue, you can begin advertising. If the band have given you press packs and biographies, talk to your local radio stations and press. You can get a good plug in the local 'What's on' pages, especially if you offer tickets as prizes. Consider producing A2, A3 and A4 posters, plus leaflets. You must be prepared to push and push your church about buying tickets – niceness does not always work. Bill the event as something that the congregation can bring non-Christian friends to – an opportunity to introduce their friends to other Christians. Also, insist on payment on delivery of the tickets, or you will be for ever chasing money!

At some point you will need to decide about food and drink. If you have chosen a venue that serves drinks, then this takes care of itself. If not, you will have to provide drinks as part of the event. You may wish to sell only soft drinks, but remember that if you decide to sell alcohol, you will need a licence to do this.

On the day itself, ensure that you are at the venue three to four hours before the event. The band might need help setting things up, moving equipment and carrying instruments. There will also be decisions to make about the venue, the layout of the tables and a myriad other things you had not considered.

During the event, be aware of what is happening around you. As the concert organizer you are responsible for all aspects of the event, including safety.

After the event, ensure that the band are paid and have everything loaded into their car or van, and that the venue is returned to its original state. In reality, you will be the last person to leave the venue other than the caretaker!

GUESTS

Being a jazz night, you will find that only people who have at least a passing interest in jazz will come to the concert. Some of your guests will be those who have responded to your advertising. Others will be the guests of your church members. You need to have at least 100 to 150 people to create the right atmosphere.

COST

The costs for this event are from the band, the hall and the advertising. The band will cost around £100 per band member – but this does depend on how famous they are! You might find that a hotel will charge you a lower rate for their room if they are allowed to sell drinks throughout the event. Your advertising costs will be mainly in printing leaflets and tickets, but this can be set against your ticket price.

VARIATIONS

I have focused on the jazz night because this is an event I have found to be fruitful and enjoyable. However, consider the following alternatives:

- Children's concerts. Jim Bailey, Ishmael, Shane Rootes, Doug Horley and Captain Alan are all great people to host a family event that is excellent for inviting non-Christian families to.

- Lunchtime concerts. Lay on light lunches (for a small cost), especially if you are in the town centre.

- Classical concerts. There are some very good classical three-, four- or five-piece 'groups'. While this is a little more specialized, there are many people who will enjoy a classical night.

- Black gospel concerts. Again, there are many non-Christians who will come to watch a great black gospel concert. Try it and see!

- Youth rock concerts. There are now some excellent rock bands and youth worship leaders who will be well accepted by the youth in your area who can put on a great concert.

At the end of the day, there is as much scope as your imagination will allow. Just let your taste run with your imagination and see what results!

OUR EXPERIENCE

We have hosted two jazz nights over the past three years with Ben Castle and his band. One was in a local hotel, in a downstairs room. The atmosphere was terrific, and we had around 130 people, of which 50 were non-Christians. For the second event we used our church hall and managed to get about 400 people along, of which around 150 were non-Christians. On both occasions we used tables seating six people. On the first night, there was a bar provided by the hotel; on the second, we provided soft drinks on the tables. Both events covered costs, and Ben shared his testimony and pushed Alpha. We have been pleased with both events on all counts.

30 Karaoke Evening

PLANNING

The first part of your planning is really to decide whether you want to do your own karaoke or go to a restaurant that has karaoke. In doing it yourself at home, you will need to provide food and drinks at your group's expense. Going to a restaurant will mean that everyone pays for their own meal, so the cost to the group will be smaller – and you do not have to worry about finding a karaoke machine. The most likely restaurant to have such a machine will be your local Chinese restaurant, as karaoke has been an Eastern phenomenon, or look in your *Yellow Pages* or *Thomson Local* directory.

If you decide to go DIY there are machines and discs available for sale on the market. However, part of the fun is to be in a good atmosphere where people do not mind making a fool of themselves.

GUESTS

It is best to invite a cross-section of individuals, some of whom will be outgoing and willing to join in quickly, and some who can ease themselves into the evening. This means that the event can start quickly and those without inhibitions will encourage the rest. Singing in front of others by yourself can cause you to be self-conscious, so be careful not to invite the very shy!

COST

Depending on how you do the event, you should be prepared to pay between £10 and £15 per head, and you should expect each person to pay. If you are doing a DIY version, then the cost will be considerably lower for everyone.

VARIATIONS

Because you are using discs with visual 'video'-style pictures, you can style your event on periods, using music and clothes as props:

- Decades (e.g. 60s.).
- Countries (e.g. USA/UK).

OUR EXPERIENCE

We have used karaoke at parties such as stag nights. It is a good clean way of having fun and getting rid of those inhibitions! It has played a part in introducing Christian and non-Christian friends, as well as in cementing relationships with existing friends.

31 Laser Quest

PLANNING

This event does not require endless hours of planning or thought. It is, however, important to book the 'arena', as they do tend to be busy places. There will also be a limit to the number of people who can play, so be sure to get firm names for the event. If people have to give a non-refundable deposit it invariably reminds them to turn up!

GUESTS

Some degree of mobility is required as the game is often played on two levels. Running, squatting and general mayhem make the game run better, so this is not a game for your great aunt's best friend! However, bearing in mind that there will be a lower age or minimum height limit, almost anyone can essentially play the game.

COST

Cost will typically be between £4 and £6 per game, which will last anywhere between 20 and 30 minutes, depending on the arrangements you make. As Laser Quest is often in the same building as other games (mostly ten-pin bowling), it will have fast-food and drink arrangements that could push the cost up. Sometimes there is a happy hour, so you might wish to plan your game for that time.

VARIATIONS

This is a team event, but you could introduce the best score for individuals or for the team. You could combine the evening with ten-pin bowling or a pool tournament (they often go together), but be careful of the costs involved.

OUR EXPERIENCE

This game has often been better attended by younger people or people with families in their teens. As there is not much time to talk during the game itself, we have found that the food and drinks have been important for social interaction and friendship-building. Costs have been reduced by hosting drinks and food at our home after the event.

32 Local Sports

PLANNING

This 'event' can take one of two options. The first revolves around you doing sport. Badminton, squash, golf and five-a-side football are all good for getting to know other people and having a great time. I now have some good friendships that have been built around sporting activities, and have found the benefits excellent (except that aching feeling the next morning!). Planning this involves agreeing with your friends a date and time, booking a court or game and going for it. As racket sports are good for mixed players, they are also a way of two couples getting to know each other well. Do not be limited by thinking that you have to stick with single-sex games, but make sure that you always include your own spouse in the games – for obvious reasons!

The second option revolves around you going to watch other people killing themselves for enjoyment! In my humble opinion this is much better for you, except where the pocket is concerned! Planning this sort of activity depends on what sport is on near you and how much you are willing to pay to watch. In my home town we have football (amateur), tennis (women and senior tournaments), cycling, motorbike racing and banger racing, cricket (county) and rugby (amateur). Then there are other one-off sporting activities that are worth going to see.

You simply need to find other like-minded people and do

it! There is plenty of time for chatting and getting to know each other. A day watching cricket can be excellent for developing relationships (and a suntan).

GUESTS

These will be any like-minded people. Since the idea of this event is to get to know non-Christians, start with your cell group and church friends and begin to reach out. Going to sporting events or playing sport is a great way of introducing your existing friends to your new ones. You never know, they might just like each other!

COST

Depends on what you do and where you go to do it. Playing sport should never cost you more than £5. Watching sport can cost a great deal, especially professional soccer. Bear in mind too that there are food and drink and parking costs to consider when setting your budget.

VARIATIONS

If you do not like sport, substitute this for theatre, music, art or shopping. Use your imagination. If you like doing something, chances are someone else will too, and you can have a great time together. Finding the opportunity should not be too hard.

OUR EXPERIENCE

Recently I had a great time with a non-Christian friend watching motorbikes going round in circles. We took the children, who thought it was fantastic, and we enjoyed ourselves chatting, laughing and shouting together. We have had

other great times since doing other activities, and our friendship is building.

Also, I love playing sport, and I find that being beaten by
my non-Christian friends is good for the soul and makes
them feel good (I am not being condescending – I simply
cannot win!). The time spent chatting afterwards is excellent,
and friendships are so easy to build this way.

33 Men Behaving Wisely/Absolutely Fabulous Night for Women

The idea here is to host an event for men or women looking at good principles for living. For ease of description, I am going to focus on the men's night.

PLANNING

As you will need a speaker for this event, you may have to consult with his diary before you set a date. The venue, too, may need booking, and I would suggest a neutral venue. The private function room of a local restaurant or pub would be ideal. Consider providing refreshments.

With regard to your speaker, choose someone who is fun and engaging, but challenging – maybe a personality speaker (actor/sportsman, etc.) or a good church minister (provided they can mix with the ordinary man on the street!).

Invite as many men as possible – the more the merrier – bearing in mind the venue's capacity. Plan to follow the speaker with some interactive discussion and mention other church activities such as Alpha.

GUESTS

As this is a men's night, you will really want all men! Try to achieve a good mix of Christians and non-Christians, as this will help keep a balance during discussions. Again, a good mix of ages will be helpful.

COST

The cost will depend on the venue and what you decide to have food-wise. You may also need to pay your speaker, and this will cost more if you invite a personality speaker. The event should be free to your guests, however, if not to members of your church.

VARIATIONS

Various topics for a men's night:

- Sport – this is especially helpful if your church has its own sports team (e.g. soccer or cricket) or has badminton/squash leagues, etc.

- Health – more men are becoming health conscious these days, and a good local Christian doctor might attract a lot of guests.

- Family – many men struggle with parenting, especially if, like me, they are often away on business. Many appreciate being offered help with their families, especially as there is a great demand on men to be 'in control' or hold it together.

- Money – a great topic if you can talk about money and how to make it!

Various topics for a women's night:

- Health – a female doctor who can speak on women's health issues may be a good idea.

- Family – many women have to cope with working and bringing up a family and some have to do so as a single parent.

- Sport – many women are very interested in sporting topics.

You will notice that the topics are the same for men and women – it's just that they need to be approached differently. I would recommend the Care for the Family videos and packs called *Parenting*. You could present one of the topics from the pack as a one-off event. You may even find that there is enough interest for you to turn the event into an ongoing short-term programme. The *Parenting* pack lends itself incredibly well to a six-week course. This would naturally need to be for men and women rather than single-sex.

Of course, you will think of many other topics to run with, and you can be as creative as you like, so long as you can hit a topic that will interest others, particularly non-Christians.

OUR EXPERIENCE

We have run a parenting course at our church for men and women, and have found it a great 'fishing' evening. Several from the course have subsequently been through Alpha. We have also hosted single-sex evenings (mainly for women), and have found interest from non-Christians, but it is important to get the subject right.

34 The Moveable Feast

If you feel that simply inviting people to a meal at your home is both boring and uneventful, try having a three-course meal, with each course in a different place. In doing so, you will give more people in your group the opportunity to be hospitable, and your guests an opportunity to see and visit the homes of a wider variety of people. This will inevitably help to relax people, and give your guests a wider view of your church.

PLANNING

If you plan this in the height of summer, you could host it in people's gardens. Alternatively, you could host it at a few of your local beauty spots. Decide on whether a host will be available to provide the food at each venue (for example, when visiting people's homes or gardens) or whether it will be more in the nature of a series of picnics, in which case food and eating utensils may need to be transportable.

Above all, keep it simple! The first course could be salad, soup or an Italian-style meat antipasto. The main course should be a barbecue, jacket potatoes, or easy-to-prepare dishes such as lasagne. The final course could be something like a gateau or cheesecake, though a good apple pie or cheese and biscuits always go down well.

If you plan carefully, you could also arrange a different activity for each spot – cricket, football, Frisbee challenge or rounders are all good family sports. Alternatively, you could try a league-style event where each person plays the same game and his or her score is carried to the final league. Of course, the winner will need to be awarded a prize!

Having sorted out where and what you will eat, you will then need to decide who will prepare the food. This may already have been decided through your discussion about what you will eat, and those who make the suggestions are likely to be those who prepare it. Others in the group can sort out the games. It is most important to have someone who will organize the timings and the administration of the day. Someone has to keep the day on line, and in my experience this cannot be a committee.

GUESTS

You will find that you can invite all sorts of people to this event. You can make this a family day, or you can limit it to a certain age group, such as over-50s. The group of people you invite will determine the sorts of venues and activities you plan.

COST

If you go for this simple format, the only expense will be in the food, which could be shared between the planning group, and there will therefore be no need to pass on the cost to your guests. Of course, if you decide on the picnic approach, you might want everyone to bring along some food to contribute to the feast.

VARIATIONS

Why not combine the day with something like a treasure hunt or an Easter egg hunt? Some other ideas would be:

- A cultural moveable picnic. (Visit some heritage sites and take time to look around them.)

- An ice-cream parlour walkabout.

- A three-parks walk (if your town has three parks!).

- A three-film day. (Go to see three different movies in three different cinemas. You could have popcorn in the first, a hot dog in the second and an ice cream in the last!)

- A coffee morning walkabout. Use several homes to visit to have coffee (with different sorts of fresh coffee to try, of course!).

35 Paintballing

PLANNING

An event like paintballing really needs planning about eight weeks in advance, primarily in order to book a local paint-balling site. To find your local site, visit your tourist information centre, or ask the local council where one might be found. Most centres will offer you a range of options from an all-day game, to a one-hour game in the evening. Do make sure that you have exclusive use of the site, otherwise you may end up playing the county short-distance rifle-shooting champion by mistake! Planning the event so early means that you can tailor your day around cost, time and availability. I recommend a one-hour game in the early evening for those who have never played before, and it is certainly the cheapest option. For the more advanced, day games with lunch provided are excellent, but they can be much more costly.

Remember that there will be an optimum number of players: too many and it is too hard; too few and it is too easy. Your centre should give you good advice in these areas.

GUESTS

Think carefully about who to invite. Paintballing is an intense energetic activity, so your invitees need to be fit and well. You will be asked to sign a disclaimer, simply because the game is fast and furious, played on rough ground or woodland, and the possibility of injury is real.

A game of mixed ages and sex works well, though some of your friends may need persuading that they really do want to be shot at with small plastic pellets of paint! Inviting a number of house groups, and telling them that they can only come if they invite a non-Christian friend, is very fruitful and leads to a good balance in the teams.

COST

A one-hour game will cost anywhere between £10 and £25, depending on where you are and how many paintballs you want to use. Prices for whole-day games will vary, depending on the size of the group, the location, number of paintballs ordered and lunch. However, you should try to keep the cost to a level where most people can afford to play, without the embarrassment of low-income people being excluded.

VARIATIONS

Remember that there is always one thing you cannot plan yourself: the weather! Paintball centres tend to be outside and as such there is always a risk, so plan an alternative for the event, just in case the weather is so poor that you wouldn't take your dog out in it!

You could always add the following activities to a paint-ball event:

- A visit to the local kebab/pizza house.

- A Chinese/Indian takeaway.

- Home for drinks and snacks.

- A visit to the pub.

Generally speaking, paintballing by itself is not enough. Because of the nature of the event, most of the guests are nervous and quiet before the game. After the game, all anyone can talk about is that great shot that took out an opponent or what cheats the opposite team are! Adding on an optional extra gives people time to chat and to get to know each other better. Having fought against and for each other, there is a strong bonding that they will want to explore. Beware though: optional extras add to the cost of the event.

FOLLOW-UP

Follow-up activities will depend largely on the make-up of the original group. Other sporting activities can be pursued, such as ten-pin bowling, Laser Quest, snooker/pool. Alternatively, low-profile meals in couples or in small groups would be very appropriate.

This sort of event is most definitely in the relationship-building area, and an invitation to Alpha may not be appropriate. On the other hand, visiting a sporting event, such as soccer or hockey, can be useful and build on the existing shared interest. Whatever you decide to do next, make sure that it is within four weeks.

OUR EXPERIENCE

We have used this activity several times now and have had a great blast! We have had people of every age involved (16–60), male and female, and of course Christians and non-Christians. It has been very successful.

36 Parents and Toddlers Events

There are many ways of reaching out to parents and toddlers, and the fact is that many churches already have good programmes for them. This chapter is included to offer suggestions to those churches that currently do not include any programmes at all, and to offer some alternatives to those that do.

PLANNING

The basic parents and toddlers programme is the one- to two-hour get-together for coffee and cakes while the children play. This activity can be held in someone's home or in a church centre. To plan this well, you do need to have plenty of toys, unbreakable furniture and an attitude that does not worry about spillages and general wear and tear. You could also provide nappies and other helpful bits that parents need.

You can begin to develop this basic concept by offering various other stimulating activities. For example, the teddy bears' picnic. You can invite your friends and their youngsters on an exciting picnic with their teddies. Food should include 'bear' food like honey. You can offer prizes for the best-dressed teddy!

Think about organizing relevant home party plans (books/toys, etc.) for parents while their youngsters play happily around them. By doing this, you can introduce good appropriate Christian literature for both parent and toddler. Have you seen the range that is currently available?

Trips out can be tremendous fun. These need only be for an hour or so, but could include visiting a local farm during lambing, a swim at the local pool, or 'keep fit' for parents and toddlers (this can be a lot of fun!).

If you have facilities, organize two activities at the same time. You could host a 'baby-sitting' area in one room while parents listen to interesting talks on such subjects as health, education, stimulating children and reading schemes in another. You might find that your local health visitor or a local primary school teacher would come in to talk to them for an hour or so. You can develop baby-sitting for short periods while the parent goes to the local supermarket or does some general housework without their normal 'help'!

If you have the abilities, you could visit parents and toddlers and offer to do some of their housework for an hour each week. Ironing, laundry and hoovering are all excellent services to offer. If you have many single parents in your location, such services can literally be a godsend, so this is an excellent way to reach out to local parents and their families.

Other things you can offer include a system of passing on clothes. Your church may already have an informal route of passing on unneeded clothing (i.e. clothes children have grown out of but not worn out!), toys, books and furniture. Perhaps you could also 'hire out' equipment like car seats. This again will help you stay close to the parents and toddlers in your area.

Finally, why not develop an 'early bird' or 'later bird' service for families with younger children of school age? With many parents working longer hours, you could offer the facility of picking up their children and dropping them off at school or picking them up from school and looking after them until their parents come home.

Many of the above can be done informally without any insurance or registration required. Such activities as baby-sitting or early birds may need to be registered with your local authority and/or insurance companies. Your local child-minding organization will be able to tell you what you need to do locally to ensure that you do not break any laws and that you remain covered by your insurance.

GUESTS

Nearly all your parents with young children will have contacts and friends with children of a similar age. This will be your immediate target area of non-Christians. There will be many parents who already have children at nursery, and you should not try to compete with the services the nurseries offer. At the end of the day you are reaching out to the parents, not providing a nursery – unless you feel that this is part of your calling in the local community. You will also find that if you offer an excellent service and keep good links with health visitors and so on, your local health authority will be keen to put other parents in contact with you.

COST

There could be some significant costs in the early period as you buy toys, paper, pencils and all the other bits you will need. To help with this your church members could donate pass-me-down clothing and equipment. There will be ongoing costs for tea, coffee, squash and biscuits, but these should not be too high. Any outings should be paid for by the parents, unless you feel that there are some who cannot afford the cost. If you have a local speaker in, you should offer to pay their costs, though many are happy to speak for free.

OUR EXPERIENCE

My own church currently offers a Friday morning drop in. This has 'baby-sitting' opportunities and we offer speakers for the parents on a wide variety of topics that they themselves have requested. From this we have had parents attending our Alpha courses, several of whom have later become Christians, and we now run several small cell groups for some of those who attend the Friday mornings.

37 Pay More, Eat Less

This event involves hosting a meal where the guests pay more money for less food and the resulting profit goes to a third world cause.

PLANNING

First of all, decide the extent of the meal and when you plan to have it. If it is to be a lunchtime meal, choose the day carefully. Obviously the aim is to reach friends and neighbours of your church, so if you hold it midweek, the response will inevitably be low. Of course, you could alleviate this by providing crèche facilities so that mothers at home can attend.

If you intend to hold the event in the evening, the scope is much wider and the likelihood of good attendance higher. It is up to you whether you make this a family affair, or limit it to adults only.

Agree on which charity you will support. It may be a church-based one or it may be an internationally known charity. If your intention is to encourage church members to bring people along, then using an organization connected to your church will help focus your church's attention. After all, now there are two reasons for supporting the event. If you intend to advertise widely and hope to have people attending whom no one in church knows, then you need to make your choice as well-known as possible. Whichever way you go, ensure that there is some connection between the 'pay more – eat less' concept and the charity you are using (in other words, try to make it an organization that provides food for the hungry).

Because people are coming to an event with a purpose, this is one time where it is acceptable to give a clear presentation: first and foremost for the charity you have chosen, and secondly for something like an Alpha course. You could even ask a bright new Christian to share their story.

As part of your early planning, decide on the menu you will offer. You could make it as basic as possible – for example soup, rice dishes and other staple foods – which will help your guests identify with the poor of the world as they pay an extortionate rate for their meal. Alternatively, you could offer things like pizzas or burgers.

Having decided the menu, agree a price for the meal, then advertise it. Make it clear which charity you are supporting and that there will be a short talk. This will mean that if someone decides to attend, they know exactly what they are coming to – this avoids problems later!

Plan the meal as though it were any other meal you would host as a church. If this is the first time you have hosted such a meal, allow plenty of time for preparation and cooking. In fact, the first time through, you might want to go for something simple like a ploughman's meal. You will need a group of people to cook and serve, and a different set of people to clear up and wash up. The tables should be set properly. You could use long tables where twelve to sixteen people can sit, or smaller ones seating four to six. Allow one and a half to two hours for the meal, depending on how many people are coming.

Make sure that if someone is talking this is restricted to 15 minutes maximum – keep it short and sharp. Most of that time should be taken with 'plugging' the charity. After all, this is the main reason people are here! Each person should leave with a leaflet about the charity and an invite to Alpha or some other outreach event you will be hosting.

If you are able to get people's names and addresses, you can then write to them thanking them for their support and reminding them of the outreach event or Alpha course you told them about. Make sure that you announce how much money you have raised through the event and tell people that they can add more money if they so wish.

Finally, your local press should be interested in a story like this, so you should invite the photographers along. This will publicize both the charity and your church.

GUESTS

Many people these days are concerned about third world matters, especially feeding the poor. Your guest list should be wide and varied, and your church members need to invite as many as possible along. Try to make it a family affair (timing will be crucial if you do). You may find that advertising in your local press will help bring in people you would not have met previously.

This may be one event your youth group will support strongly, and you may want to make it age-specific so that local schools and colleges will be interested.

COST

The cost of this event is in the food and drink you provide and the advertising. It is up to you whether or not you extract these costs from the money you raise. I would suggest not as this can be deflating for the people at the event. If you can, underwrite the event from your church budget. Obviously the more extravagant you get, the higher the cost will be.

VARIATIONS

You could run the same event, but ask people to bring cans of food, children's wear and other non-perishable gifts that you can send to a third world country. You could also choose one particular country and offer food from that country. In one case, a church decided to run this event for Bangladesh, and asked the local curry house to cook an authentic Bangladeshi meal for the people who attended. The curry house owner offered his services and food free of charge as part of the event. You can imagine how much local press coverage this achieved!

38 Personality Speaker

PLANNING

The very first thing to do when planning a well-known speaker is to contact their agent or publisher. Most publishers/music companies will put you in touch with the agent, who will give you the details you require. The most important details are how much the speaker will cost and when they are available. The answers to these two questions will determine all the other parts of the planning process.

Cost is very important. Many Christians hold the view that everything involved in the kingdom should be free. Patently this is not so. The more well known the 'star' is, the greater the cost will be – and the harder it will be to book them. Most Christian 'stars' will charge considerably less than their secular counterparts, but do not be surprised to be asked to pay for the evening's entertainment. The author of this book, however, will be happy to be booked for the price of a curry and the latest Terry Pratchett novel!

One way round this is the author tour. If a well-known star has a new book out, the publishing house will be looking for opportunities to 'place' their author on a speaking tour. It is likely that at this point you could book an author while they are effectively being subsidised by the publishing house. In order for this to be a reality, you should contact houses such as Kingsway, Hodder, and HarperCollins (have a look around your local Christian bookshop to get the wide range available) to see what they are planning. You will need to construct a good case for why the author should come to your particular church (numbers attending, style of event, publicity available, etc.).

If you have a good relationship with your local Christian bookshop, then together you could put on an excellent event (this will help you subsidise the event even further, as the bookshop will be involved financially too). If they are in doubt, there are many bookshops already doing some sterling work, and the publishing houses will put you in touch to get some better idea of what to do.

So, assuming that the idea now has some legs and you are beginning to put together a plan for such an event, the question really is who to invite. You could go for a high-profile person from the sporting world or the world of TV (e.g. Jonah Lomu or Sally Magnusson). You could choose well-known TV stars like Bobby Ball or Sid Little, or authors who have a good name outside the church. Other well-known people who will attract non-Christians are Rosemary Conley or Fiona Castle. Choosing the right person will shape your event. Even an author little known outside the Christian publishing world can be attractive if the subject is right (parenting, finance, etc.).

Because of who they are, the date of the event will be determined by their diaries. Once you have a price and a date, you can book the venue, and then you can prepare the publicity – lots of it! Bearing in mind that you could be paying a lot of money for your guest, don't skimp on your marketing. Involve the local press (give free tickets for competitions, etc.) and radio stations (you can often get tapes of the speaker speaking to give some idea of how interesting they are). Place adverts in the right places, thinking about who will want to come to listen. Will the majority of listeners be male, or female? Will most people want to come, or will it be targeted to a limited number of people? You will then need to prepare A3 posters and A5 leaflets (these could be from the same artwork, thus saving cost).

Sometimes it is right to take this sort of event away from the church. Try booking a hotel function room or a whole restaurant (the proprietors will be interested in advertising as well then), or even a sports club if your speaker is from the world of sport. Be creative in your venue and you will be able to reach a wider number of people. In an event like this, numbers are very important – not only in recouping your costs, but also in exposing as many people as possible to the 'story'.

Finally, make sure that you understand the needs of the speaker. Will they need a hotel room for the evening? Will they need meals? Do they have a press pack and what will they want you to say about them? Are you paying for one person, or will there be an entourage? These questions need dealing with early so that there are no surprises!

On the night itself, have plenty of stewards and helpers available, and assign one encouraging and helpful person to look after your speaker. This should not be you if you are organizing the event, as you will be very busy for the whole night. You should ensure that there is adequate PA and that you have music (in the form of a CD) as people enter and leave. If the speaker is an author have copies of their book(s) available, and check beforehand whether they are happy to sign copies. Finally, find out whether your speaker is happy to talk to members of the audience, especially as the audience will want to ask all sorts of questions. If they are happy, announce a question and answer time.

Be as helpful and as courteous as possible to your speaker, and make sure that all their needs are met, but remember that this is your event, and you should have one or two clear leaflets available advertising forthcoming events held by your church, and something about the church itself. If the event is directly evangelistic, make sure that there are some people available to share the gospel and talk to seekers, but do not crowd the event with too many announcements, and do not, under any circumstances, be tempted to re-preach the speaker's message!

GUESTS

Invite as many personal guests through your church members as possible, targeting the right sort of people and age group. Your publicity should draw many other interested people. Try to get their names and addresses and write to them thanking them for their attendance and offering other events for their interest.

COST

The two major costs are the speaker themselves (including their food and accommodation) and the venue cost. The cost of publicity will be small by comparison. Be prepared to charge for admission – the better known the speaker, the more you can charge! If you choose to hold the event in a restaurant, you could make it very exclusive by charging a lot and expecting fewer people, effectively having an after-dinner speaker!

VARIATIONS

These will depend on the speaker you decide to book. For example, if the speaker is a sports personality, book yourself into a sports club (gym, etc.) or games club (soccer/cricket, etc.). You could try theme nights tied into food, or an issues night with a debate afterwards. (If you do this, be provocative in your choice of debate so that you get good conversation and discussion.) You could try an election-style debate around a local or national election. Whatever you do, book a venue and food in accordance with the person who is speaking, otherwise you will miss the opportunity to tie in local business or free publicity.

OUR EXPERIENCE

A church connected to ours has hosted such events and had particular success with Rosemary Conley and Fiona Castle. There was a good turn-out and a lot of interest was shown. Converting that interest has been hard work, but well worth the effort.

39 The Picnic

PLANNING

Simply set a date and go for it. Either ask each individual family to bring their own food, or – which is more fun – arrange for each family to bring a part of the picnic (e.g. salad, meat, bread). We have found that picnics arranged as after church events have worked well, as there are larger numbers of people able to come. In addition, because they are coming to the picnic, it is a good way of encouraging non-Christians to attend church. Finally, you can always have a picnic indoors in the church hall if necessary.

Organize some games for people to play if they want to – otherwise they can just sit and chat. Soccer, cricket and rounders are the obvious ones, but why not try a Frisbee wide game (two goals like soccer, but throwing a Frisbee around) or a well-planned treasure hunt for the children?

GUESTS

Anyone and everyone is welcome on a picnic and, with organized games, all can join in. In reality, this is an excellent cross-generational event that is inclusive of all who go.

COST

Cost is minimal, as the only thing you should really pay for is the food and drink (and ice creams!).

VARIATIONS

A good picnic need not have many new ideas, but just in case you are getting bored with the usual, try:

- Food variations (e.g. Chinese, Indian or vegetarian.)

- A good walk or country ramble before eating.

- A picnic followed by a swimming session.

- A picnic for meeting the families after child baptisms, etc.

OUR EXPERIENCE

We have found that this is the easiest and quickest event to organize and allows plenty of time for chatting. Nobody feels threatened, and we have successfully combined it with church attendance by non-Christian families. Do not despise the humble picnic!

40 Play Station Night

How many people in your church have access to a Play Station? Probably more than you think. Further, the age range of the people who play the games is wider than you think. Many people into their 20s and 30s are hooked on Play Stations.

PLANNING

An evening with a Play Station will not be hard to organize, but it may be hard to limit the numbers of people who can participate! In essence, the room is free and easy to book (playing at home), the hardware will be supplied by someone in your church, and the games will come on the night. What could be easier?

Simply arrange an evening, make sure you have the hardware, and invite your guests! However, you could make it more complicated than this. You could hold it in your church hall and play the games on a big screen so that all can watch! You could organize competitions based on one game (say football), with knockout games and a grand final. If it is football you are playing, why not insist that 'players' come in their chosen team strip (certainly the shirt)? You could organize leagues with different games, or a fantasy league with prizes. You could do a lot to make this event much more interesting than simply turning up and playing.

Of course, you must also keep the interest of those not

playing the current game, so, as most people who come will be addicts of the games, you could provide 'warm-up facilities' with PC games, extra Play Stations or Game Boys! You will also want to provide food and drink, and this could be made to be varied and interesting.

GUESTS

Your guests will be of different ages and sexes, but they'll have something in common: they'll be addicted! Invite as many people as you wish, provided your house can cope and you have enough other games to keep your friends interested. Lots of music, lots of noise and a great atmosphere will mean that people will really enjoy themselves. One way of keeping interest and involving everyone is to ask them to bring their favourite game to review.

COST

The only cost involved is the food and drink. If you provide this yourself the cost won't be very high, although if you decide to have a takeaway this will inevitably rise.

VARIATIONS

Try Game Boy or PC games as outlined above. Alternatively, you could ask a local supplier to your home to demo the latest hardware and games to a group of interested people. The supplier should be very interested in your idea as he could increase his market.

OUR EXPERIENCE

Our experience of this sort of idea has been at the individual level, where people in church have invited their Christian and non-Christian friends to an informal evening of Play Station. This has proved to be helpful in building friendships at the individual level. We have yet to host a small group party for Play Station addicts.

41 'Pub Quiz'

PLANNING

While I have called this the pub quiz, you can easily put on a quiz night in your local church hall or hire a smallish room for the evening. There are many suitable CD-ROMs that now give you lots of questions and answers, so you don't have to spend time working everything out. There are also many books on the market that will give you as much help as you need. Don't invite non-Christian guests and then give them a Bible quiz. I know this sounds obvious, but it has happened! You will need to organize several groups to get together for this. Rivalry is usually high, so be prepared for some 'fun' on the night! You will need plenty of drinks (arguing can be thirsty work!) and some prizes. You will also need plenty of room and chairs for the evening. As a variation, you could invite your friends to help you form a local pub quiz team – great fun if you can take two or three groups along and show how stupid you really are!

GUESTS

These will usually be adults. You will have great success with those who think they know it all, i.e. most of us. Nearly all who join in will enjoy themselves, particularly the Trivial Pursuit experts. If you vary the night (see below), then you might want a more clearly defined guest list, but in general terms invite everyone you know!

COST

Cost will be minimal. The cost of a CD-ROM will be around £10 and quiz books around £7. If held in a church hall, then the only cost will be your drinks, and a well-made non-alcoholic punch will be greatly appreciated.

VARIATIONS

- Sports quiz night.
- Film quiz night.
- Music quiz night.

OUR EXPERIENCE

Inviting guests was the hardest part of staging a quiz night. We also found that the event needs to be well organized on the night. It is important that the quiz master keeps the evening moving and the arguing to a minimum. They have to be well disciplined in order to keep noise and cheating under control and the jokes need to move fast. A confident and quick-witted person is required. Guests have enjoyed the event. Time was allowed afterwards for general chatting and friendship-building.

42 Rambles and Walks

PLANNING

Once you have decided how long the walk is going to be and where it will take place, this will determine whether it will be an early evening stroll or a day-long ramble. The alternatives will depend on where you live. You may be fortunate enough to be surrounded by beautiful countryside with many superb walks. If you live in the inner city, there won't be so many choices, but why not, for example, engage the services of a local historian and walk around the historical highlights of the town/city, learning as you get fit!

A word of caution: you will always be told by keen walkers that the walk they are suggesting is 'not that far'. This usually entails a ten-mile hike with only Kendal mint cake for survival!

Walks are ideal for family occasions, and it is great fun to let the children go off in front (where you can still see them!) and chat as you go along. What could be more enjoyable than a good two-mile stretch of the legs in the morning, followed by a picnic beside a river before the walk back? In your planning, therefore, make sure that you have thought about little legs as well (a ten-mile hike becomes inappropriate at that point!).

You could always have the option of walking to a particular place that has a restaurant or pub, but bear in mind that a walk should be cheap and accessible to all. Another option is to drive into the hills to meet up for a good day out.

GUESTS

If you choose an early evening stroll, then be aware that people with young families will have time constraints. A good day's ramble might not appeal to everyone, but most people will appreciate an invite to a nice walk and picnic.

COST

Keep it as low as possible! In fact, for the price of a picnic, a gallon of petrol and a few cans of coke, you can have a hugely enjoyable day.

VARIATIONS

•   Historical walks around your town.

•   Nature trails.

•   Visits to National Trust and parkland areas.

•   Combining walking with a treasure hunt (keeps the children's interest).

OUR EXPERIENCE

In the early days of our church starting up, we used to go out into the hills for a walk together over the bank holidays. This enabled us to grow together as a church very quickly, and it meant that we were able to bring friends and relations to a very low-key introduction to the church on neutral ground. We made many good contacts over this period.

   We have continued to have walks as individual cell/home groups and in bigger groups of cells. Our 20s groups often go for walks that incorporate visitors, and these have been great at cementing relationships with new people. We have also found that if you have people simply turn up on Sunday morning, they are often very willing to go for a walk in the afternoon with a group of people.

We have found these simple events easy to organize, easy to invite people to and great for building new bridges.

43 Sale of Skills

Everyone needs some help from time to time, and sometimes people are prepared to pay for that help, especially if the money is going to a good cause. So why not hold an auction for people's time and skills, and donate all the money to a good local or international cause?

PLANNING

For this to succeed, you need first to get members of your church to donate their time or skills. Such skills as decorating, carpentry, DIY, gardening and car maintenance are very useful. It is important to remind people that if someone is paying for a service – even if the person doing the work is not receiving the money – they will expect a good deal. Buyers will not be impressed if they buy decorating skills only to find that the decorator cannot hang wallpaper straight!

Time is also a very valuable commodity, and people may well be willing to pay for domestic services like ironing, washing-up or hoovering. Think about all the chores you have to do and the luxury of having someone else do them for you! These are the sorts of things that others will pay for.

Decide which good cause you will donate the money to and then, if you are brave or have a super salesman in your group, you might like to get local businesses involved. They can donate time or services. Supermarkets can offer vouchers or special deals. Garages can offer a free MOT or service. McDonald's are often willing to offer vouchers for good causes. Your local bookshop could offer books. The sorts of deals you can come up with are only limited by your vision and creativity. Remember, the more that is donated, the more buzz you can create!

Once you have collected all the available skills and time you can find, set a date for the auction and find a venue. A church hall or community centre would be a great venue. Having done this, start to invite your guests. If you are donating all proceeds to a local charity, your local newspaper should run a news story and may even advertise for free. If you have many local businesses involved, you will probably find the newspapers falling over themselves to help. You may also find that your local radio will plug the event.

There should be a good period between the invites going out and the event itself. Just like all auctions, you may need to publish a listing of the offers, maybe in a leaflet. In fact, this is a good idea because it helps people plan their money, and it offers you 'advertising' space. This space should tell people about the charity you are working with and what they do. You should also keep some space in the leaflet to tell people about your church, and possibly advertise your Alpha course.

On the day it is very important to have an engaging auctioneer. If you have one in your church, get them to donate their time. If not, get the most charismatic person you can find (character-wise!) to lead the event. The more relaxed people are, the more they will buy, so this is the most important part of the function. Auctioneers need to describe what they are selling, so the 'goods' need to be on show wherever possible. The idea is to help people spend money for your charity, so do not be embarrassed by the thought of extracting money – your guests would not have come if they did not want to spend money in this way.

Allow time in the programme to tell your guests about the charity, and your church. Do not thrust the gospel at them.

Remember that this event is an attraction. Make sure that there are sufficient members of your group or church at the event so that they can engage people in conversation and develop contacts. To that end, have a coffee time either mid way or at the end of the event so that you can meet people.

Make a decision as to when payment should be made. I suggest this is at the point of purchase, so that you are not for ever trying to chase money. The purchaser and the person offering services or time should agree when the 'goods' will be delivered, and this should be as soon as possible after the event. It is advisable to make a list through the evening of who has bought what so that there are no mistakes later. Your whole event could be destroyed by people paying for services that are never delivered or are forgotten about.

Finally, try to keep a running total so that the amount of money raised can be announced at the end of the auction. You may even want to hand over a cheque there and then. This will make a good impact and provide a focal point. People will leave on a high note, and the desire to repeat the event will be high.

GUESTS

First of all, your guests should be drawn from friends and family of your church members. However, the more people you can get to come along, the better the atmosphere will be. This will lead to more money being raised and more contacts to follow. If you are well organized, you should get the names and addresses of everyone who attends, with a view to writing to them afterwards. In the letter you could tell them how much was raised, and you could also tell them about your church and perhaps invite them to a guest service or Alpha supper. If you hold the event near Christmas, why not invite them to your Christmas guest service?

COST

The cost of the event will be the coffee you provide, the hire of the hall and the cost of advertising (leaflets and posters, etc.). Remember that the aim is to give money away, not spend it. So keep your costs as low as possible.

VARIATIONS

Try a sports theme or a garden theme. With the latter, your local garden centre may be willing to host the event and offer free advertising – after all, they are trying to get people in through their doors! You may wish to have a food theme – selling meals or cakes, etc. Again, try to involve a local industry or retailer.

Above all, be as creative as you can. Planning can be as much fun as the event itself.

44 Scalextric Evening

PLANNING

Don't be fooled into thinking that this event is one for the boys. There are as many girls who will want to prove their Scalextric skills over the aggressive male as there are on the roads outside my office window!

You should allow around six weeks to plan this event. Plan the date and venue and time to make sure that you have enough track and cars that work.

About one week before the event, set up the track to ensure that everything is working. If it isn't, you have time to try different layouts or fix the parts that do not work. Double-check that everything is working on the day itself.

In addition, you need to work out a system that allows your guests time on the track throughout the evening – a round robin league followed by semi-finals and finals would work.

Once the track is up, you might want to let two or three cell groups have events through the week. In doing so, you could end the week with a bigger final event with prizes.

As an alternative to doing everything yourself, most towns have hobby shops that have Scalextric tracks already set up and are willing to hire them out by the hour or evening. If they do not, they will almost certainly know of someone in town who does. Check this out if you have no track or don't want to set up your own event.

GUESTS

Mostly grown-up men trying to regain their youth ('Do you remember when they brought out . . . ?') and women trying to upset said male protagonists! As to numbers, they will be limited to the number of tracks and cars you have as no one likes to sit out for too long – watching can be boring! Try to restrict numbers to no more than eight to ten people on any one night.

COST

If you are planning to put the event on with track that belongs to you, the only cost will be any food and drink you have at the event. I suggest a huge Chinese takeaway.

    If you choose to use a hired track, then the cost may be more limiting, but not excessive – probably around £5 per person.

VARIATIONS

You could try train set-ups and other such hobby 'toys'.

FOLLOW-UP

An event such as this allows a lot of time for chatting and building up friendships and could eventually lead to an invitation to Alpha.

OUR EXPERIENCE

We should have checked beforehand that the track worked! It didn't! So we spent most of the evening standing around chatting while someone tried to fix it – all to no avail. However, with a Chinese meal attached, the evening was not a complete disaster, and the overall feeling was that we should try it again. Our non-Christian friends got to know other Christians, and the aim of the evening was thus achieved.

45 Televised Sports Evening

The aim here is to host an evening around a major sporting event such as the World Cup or FA Cup Final. If a local team is involved, all the better. Many clubs and pubs hold such events, so yours has to offer something rather different. As a church, we should be able to offer a smoke-, alcohol- and swearing-free atmosphere that parents will feel comfortable bringing little Johnny to. You will be amazed at how many parents are looking for such events for the family! During the World Cup in 1998, quite a few churches tried this event with some success, and while the logistics seem difficult, the whole church can get behind this.

PLANNING

In the first instance, you cannot have 50 people watching their favourite sport on a 14-inch screen. You need to have the size of screen appropriate to the number of people you invite. If you host the event in your home with only ten to twelve people, you will get away with a small home TV. In the larger context, you will need to hire a bigger TV, or even a video screen. Your local *Yellow Pages* will give you phone numbers of electronic hire companies that can provide you with all you need – screens, projectors, sound systems, etc.

You will also need to lay on drinks and snacks. At home you will be able to provide bags of crisps and bottles of coke, but in the larger context perhaps you could provide such things for sale, as this will help finance your event.

In terms of planning, this should start as early as possible, as hire companies book out their equipment well in advance, and invitations need to go out before people have made other arrangements. Be as lavish as you dare – the better the event, the more people will be involved and risk inviting someone. You could advertise this event in the local newspaper, but if you do, make sure your planning is clear and well executed (or you will be!).

Above all, plan your event for the actual day and time the sporting event in question takes place. This may sound obvious, but mistakes have been known to happen! Finally, check that the building you are in has a relevant TV licence – you have been warned!

GUESTS

Families are key to this event. Lots of small boys and big boys together makes for a great atmosphere, and mothers will keep everyone in line!

COST

This could be a very expensive event to put on if you go for the 'big one'. If done in the home, it need cost very little. You have to decide which to go for. My advice is to start small and work upwards. In these days of the cell group, you could have many small events happening at the same time around your town.

VARIATIONS

The variations depend upon which sport or other type of event your cell group prefers:

• Football (FA Cup, World Cup, European Champions League, etc.).

- Grand Prix racing.

- Rugby world cup.

- Cricket world cup (for the patient among you!).

- Music – live concerts, etc.

- Royal weddings and funerals.

- Major events such as the eclipse (you have another 70 years to plan for the next one, but you know what I mean!).

OPTIONAL EXTRAS

- Drinks and snacks.

- A half-time talk on a very relevant aspect of the gospel. Don't make it full of clichés. If you are going to do this, tell your guests beforehand so that they can choose not to attend if they so wish.

- Tracts from Christians in Sport, etc. that will communicate to your guests. There are also some excellent books written by sports heroes from many different sports that will fit the event you are hosting.

FOLLOW-UP

Try booking a sports person through Christians in Sport to come and share their life story and the gospel. Many are willing to talk for a small fee, and you will be able to target your audience depending on the sport represented. The telephone number of Christians in Sport is: 01865 311211.

OUR EXPERIENCE

Just recently we hosted a football evening. We erected a
12′ × 8′ white screen and hired a very good TV projector. In
all we had around 120 people present, young and old,
Christian and non-Christian. We rigged the sound through
our normal Sunday morning PA. The atmosphere was good,
everyone seemed to enjoy themselves and the feeling was
that it was a great success. In part this was due to the fact that
a small number of people circulated around the room,
talking to people and generally making them feel at home.
We also showed videos of the best goals and the funniest
incidents, helping to create atmosphere.

46 Ten-Pin Bowling

PLANNING

When you have agreed the date you wish to play and you know how many people want to take part, you will need to book the relevant number of lanes.

GUESTS

Because all ten-pin bowling clubs are anxious to include children or less-abled people, they will probably have lane aids available for your group. This makes it an ideal pastime for families, mixed age groups and disabled groups. Most bowling lanes are set up for a maximum of six people, so try to work in multiples of six. Most alleys provide food and drink, so you could make a bigger event if you wished (see below).

COST

The cost of ten-pin bowling is entirely dependent on how many games you play, not on the number of people playing. Typically, you should pay between £3 and £5 per game. Very often there are cheap off-peak times that could help if you have families or less well off people in your party. You would increase the cost by including fast food and drinks. Some alleys will put on a buffet for you if you want to push the boat out!

VARIATIONS

Try making it a team game rather than an individual game by pitting lanes against each other – playing for each other brings a new dimension to the evening. Alternatively, you could make it highly competitive, with prizes for the best results. If you do this, make sure that there are prizes for each age group because it is embarrassing when a ten-year-old beats you. Trust me, I know!

Further, you could combine ten-pin bowling with Laser Quest, as they often tend to be in the same building.

OUR EXPERIENCE

We have found this a great cell-group activity which most people not only want to join in with, but they're happy to invite their friends. In fact it is one of the least intimidating events we have put on, and it helps build good friendships. It is also one of the easiest events to organize at short notice.

47 Theme Night

PLANNING

First of all, decide as a group what the theme of the night is going to be. An easy theme is a Chinese night as food, costume and music are easily identifiable and readily available. However, the danger in an event like this is that there is always someone who does not like the food or has some other problem with the event. If you are having home-made food, good planning is essential to ensure that you do not all bring the same dish (rice is nice with other dishes, but it can be a little overwhelming by itself).

GUESTS

To some extent this will be determined by the theme of the evening. Most people, including families and disabled people, can enjoy nationality themes. A film theme could be tricky, though not impossible, but a Delia Smith night might be very taxing for all concerned ('So, how *do* you boil an egg?'). This is a great night to invite your next-door neighbours to – everyone enjoys food.

COST

If you decide to cook all the food between you, the cost will be minimal – and you could make it more enjoyable by cooking in groups. If you decide to buy in all the food, it could get very expensive.

VARIATIONS

Here are just some of the options available for this event:

- Chinese night: the food is obvious and readily available.

- Indian night: this will limit you to guests who like spicy food.

- Irish night: the music is easily available, and with some help so are the dishes.

- Mexican night: again there may be limitations because of food taste, but grand nachos with sour cream, chillies and double-cooked beans make a great ice-breaker!

- Spanish night: bring on the paella.

- French night.

- Film night: how about a *Star Wars* intergalactic evening (even my inedible offering could be thought to be a Sith breakfast)?

- Sports night.

- Music night: food on a musical theme could be fun. (What about Sugar Plum Fairy cakes or an 1812 chilli con carne?)

If you have people in your church from the nationality involved it will add authenticity to the night and will help break down any barriers there might be (but do not bring droids, as conversation could be difficult). If this is an option, then a short talk could be given about culture and food. This will have quite an impact if the person is able to tell their story. All sorts of questions and discussion could arise.

OUR EXPERIENCE

We have held theme events such as 'A night at the pictures', and have found that most fun-loving people enjoy getting dressed up for the evening and letting their hair down. It is a great way of seeing people in a completely new light!

48 Variety Show

There are many people in your church who have talents you have not yet spotted, and who have friends who are also talented. These talents will be wide and varied: there will be singers, musicians, dancers, mime artists, ventriloquists, comedians. . . . A regular variety show in the making! So why not give them an opportunity to shine? Your variety show will give people the chance to show off their talents and to reach out to their friends.

PLANNING

First, decide on a date and book a hall with a stage. Secondly, decide on the charity you may like to support. Thirdly, talk to your friends and get them to agree to show off their talents in public. You will need to allow plenty of time for people to get used to the idea and to practise. After all, you want a fair degree of competence on the night! Also, ask your church members to invite their friends to participate. This will give you a chance to increase the range of talents on show and invite more people. I suggest you hold an audition so that you can 'weed out' the weaker acts.

Having decided who will be participating on the night, continue to encourage them, making sure that they are working on their acts. Aim to hold a dress rehearsal at least two weeks before the evening so that those who need to work harder are aware of their weaknesses!

Organize plenty of publicity. This should include details

of the local charity you are supporting on the night, and the cost of the tickets. It is also advisable to advertise what the acts are likely to be so that people know what they are coming to. Because you are giving the takings to a local charity, your local newspapers should be interested in the event and what you are doing.

Finally, you will need a small number of people to take tickets, give out programmes and help people find their seats on the night. You may need some people to hand out drinks and snacks at the end. Get someone to be in charge of the PA and possibly work out some lighting for you. You may also need someone to do some make-up for your acts!

GUESTS

Anyone who has a friend or relative in the cast will be interested. If you have young children involved, their parents will be delighted to come and watch their prodigy on stage! You will also find some people coming out of curiosity, and the better the fare, the more people will turn up on the night. Of course, you should encourage the church to invite as many people as possible.

COST

Most of the cost will be in the hall hire. If you have an adequate church hall, then you could use this. Other costs will depend on the food and drinks you offer, and the publicity you undertake.

VARIATIONS

Children

You could put on some very good productions using the younger elements of your church. There are some excellent musical plays available for children across the age ranges and these can be offered with just singing and music or they can have more varied fayre (e.g. dance, mime, readings). These are ideal for festive times such as Christmas and Easter, but are also good for other notable church calendar events such as Mother's Day.

If you run a holiday club, you could rehearse for a whole week and put on an excellent production that is fun and educational but also reaches out to the parents. Many parents will turn up to see their child in a play when they will not come to your church for any other reason.

Young people

Your youth group could put on a good musical play that they and their peers would enjoy. The more they involve their friends the better, and you could introduce the idea of a live band to go with the play. Again, parents and friends love coming to such plays.

Adults

The idea of a variety show can be daunting to some, laughable to others. However, you can dress it as a talent show. You could also put on some good musical productions of your own using available materials.

OUR EXPERIENCE

Some years ago, the church my wife and I were attending agreed to put on an Easter musical. We wrote most of the lyrics and music from within the church, rehearsed regularly for several months, and put on an excellent and interesting evening. The church rallied round with props, actors, musicians, make-up artists, stewards and car-park attendants. Both adults and children were involved, and the whole church got behind the concept. At the time there were only

80 to 100 adults in the church, so everyone had a part to play. We managed to fill a hall that held 300 people on two nights. The response was huge, and as a church we felt that we had achieved many of our targets.

I do believe that hosting such events is possible, but that the concept has to be well sold to the church in the first instance.

49 Wine-Tasting Evening

PLANNING

As alcohol can be a controversial area in some churches, you may need to check with your church leaders whether this would be approved of or not. Any alcohol consumption is frowned upon in some churches, but even where it isn't, there may be those who are reformed alcoholics, and you must be careful not to use your freedom to accidentally bring others down. Further, you must be extremely careful of the driving laws: do not drink and drive. You can imagine the headlines in your local newspaper: 'Vicar drunk in charge of staggering flock shock!'

Having said that, many church attendees are happy to participate in drinking wine, and would appreciate someone educating them in choosing the best wines. If you have the right connections, it may be possible to persuade one of your local supermarkets or wine-sellers to 'sponsor' the event by providing tasting bottles or even an expert. Here in the south east, we are fortunate to have two excellent wine-tasting centres within easy distance and they are more than willing to host such an event on their premises.

The event really needs one large room and enough glasses for the people attending. You will also need quantities of water, as cleaning glasses and palates between bottles is essential. You may also want to provide some food/snacks for the evening.

GUESTS

Anyone over 18, except those who may have a moral problem with alcohol as described above. If the wine you are tasting is really good, give me a call so that I can assess how successful your evening has been!

COST

There will be some cost involved with this event. The most inexpensive bottle of wine is now £2.99 (less than that and you will not be able to taste anything else afterwards!), and the price for a half-reasonable bottle climbs from £5 upwards. If you are being 'sponsored' then the costs may go down, depending on the arrangement you make, but you might want to encourage your group to share the cost. Adding snacks will obviously increase the cost.

VARIATIONS

The options here centre on the wine itself:

- Wine from one particular country (e.g. Australia, France, New World, Bulgaria – even England!).

- Cider-tasting. Do you know how many different ciders and perrys there are?

FOLLOW-UP

Remember that the idea of the evening is to reach non-Christians – not to focus solely on the wine-tasting! This event allows for discussion on 'Should Christians drink?' and other matters, allowing you to widen the conversation to introduce the gospel! You may use this in the run up to your Alpha course, as it will help dispel some cultural myths: 'I hadn't realized how normal you all were!'

50 Writers' Workshop

The idea behind this event is to host a workshop for budding writers and poets in your area. It has been said that everyone has at least one book in them! If you ask around your groups, you too will find that within them there are budding novelists and poets. This event is designed to bring some of these people together, along with their friends, to learn a little more about the art of writing.

PLANNING

To plan this event decide on a date and venue, and invite a trusted speaker. In most towns there are local writers who would be willing to come and help you. There are also groups in most towns that meet on a regular basis to help each other. With some investigation, you will be able to find such groups. Very often they will be willing to assist. Further, many local colleges and secondary schools will have teachers who write and would be willing to help, or there may even be a fairly well-known local author who would attend.

As part of the evening, you could arrange for food and drinks if you so wish. In addition, you could organize a reading of well-known writers. You should also arrange to meet on a regular basis afterwards to encourage each other. In doing so, you should certainly read each other's works and provide helpful, positive critiques.

GUESTS

Many of the people who want to attend this event will have an interest in literature and will have friends who are also interested. This will be your first point of contact. However, you should advertise the evening in the press, as you may find others who would like to attend. This is a great way to meet new friends.

COST

The cost of the venue should be very little, as a home will be the best place – unless you have a huge attendance. The cost should therefore be limited to simple food and drinks, and if you do have a guest speaker, you should offer them a gift for speaking – perhaps about £20 to £30 for the evening.

VARIATIONS

As poetry and lyrics are closely linked, you could host a songwriting evening for lyricists. Alternatively, you could host an evening for those who are lovers of the classics. A Charles Dickens night (or any other famous author) could be very popular.

Some Useful Addresses

The UK Christian Handbook published by Christian Research would be an invaluable directory of Christian organizations and contacts for your church. However, here are a few selected addresses that may be helpful.

Act for Christ
Ground Floor Mission House
34a High Street
Yatton
Bristol
B549 4JA

Practical help for Christians using drama; workshops, training, writing, mission preparation.

Arts in Mission
24 Yorkshire Place
Warfield Green
Bracknell
RG42 3XE

Encouraging and equipping Christian artists; assisting church in mission.

Association of Christian Writers
74 Longleaze
Wootton Bassett
Swindon
SN4 8AS

Providing advice workshops and forums for Christian writers from beginner to professional.

Baly's Cream Jazz
13 Travers Walk
Bristol
BS34 8XW

Six piece jazz band for churches and private functions.

Care for the Family
Garth House
Leon Avenue
CARDIFF
CF4 7RG

Providing support for families through seminars and resources.

Christians in Sport
PO Box 93
Oxford
OX2 7YP

Reaching the world of sport for Christ.

Frances Clarke
274a Harborne Park Road
Harborne
Birmingham
B17 0BL

Professional dancer, choreographer, dance teacher; sharing the Christian faith through dance in worship, evangelism, workshops.

Fellowship of Christian Magicians
91 Green Street
Middleton
Manchester
M24 2TB

Proclaiming the gospel using illusion and other visual aids.

Dave Hopwood – Author and Mime Artist
Christ Church
Church Street East
Woking
GU21 1YG

Training in expressing the gospel through mime, street theatre, scripts, novel writing, crafts and watercolour.

Radius (The Religious Drama Society for Great Britain)
Christ Church and Upton Chapel
1a Kennington Road
LONDON
SE1 7QP

Supporting religious drama production through training, advice, play supplies and lending library.

Soapbox
3 Bank Buildings
149 High Street
Cranleigh
Surrey
GU6 8BB

Drama workshops/seminars encouraging and developing skills with church-based drama groups.

TEAR Fund
100 Church Road
Teddington
TW11 8QE

The Evangelical Alliance Relief Fund, 'Eat Less – Pay More' projects.

Some Useful Books

Arts in Mission Resource Directory, Bible Society, ISBN 0 56404 076 2.

Becoming a Contagious Christian by Hybels & Mittelberg, Willow Creek Association, ISBN 1 89893 860 1.

Bruce & Stan's Guide to God by Bickel & Jantz, Harvest House Publishers, ISBN 1 56507 563 3.

The Church Down Our Street by Michael Wooderson, Monarch Publications, ISBN 1 85424 031 5.

Evangelism Explosion by D. James Kennedy, Tyndale House, ISBN 0 84230 764 8.

Good News Down the Street by Michael Wooderson, Grove Books, ISBN 1 85174 114 3.

How to Design & Make Banners by Banbury & Dewar, Burns & Oates, ISBN 0 85532 681 6.

How to Be Unbelievably Friendly by Chris Storey, Kingsway Publications, ISBN 0 85476 830 0.

Natural Evangelism by J. John, Lion, ISBN 0 74593 389 0.

Questions of Life by Nicky Gumbel, Kingsway Publications, ISBN 0 85476 591 3.

Storytelling – a Practical Guide by Lance Pierson, Scripture Union, ISBN 1 85999 094 0.

Telling Others by Nicky Gumbel, Kingsway Publications, ISBN 0 85476 741 X.